1974

S0-BBT-285

3 0301 00027818 0

Twayne's United States Author's Series

Sylvia E. Bowman, *Editor*

INDIANA UNIVERSITY

Amélie Rives
(Princess Troubetzkoy)

AMÉLIE RIVES
(PRINCESS TROUBETZKOY)

By WELFORD DUNAWAY TAYLOR

University of Richmond

 217

Twayne Publishers, Inc. :: New York

FOR MR. AND MRS. ALLEN RIVES POTTS,
WORTHY KINSMEN

Preface

When Amélie Rives Troubetzkoy is mentioned by literary historians, it is usually in connection with *The Quick or the Dead?* (1888). This novel has been cited by Clarence Gohdes as a significant example of the "semierotic" genre which gave impetus to the Realistic movement (*The Literature of the American People*, 741) and by James D. Hart for having first "brought popularity to some more sophisticated treatments of moral issues in high society" (*The Popular Book*, 199). Also frequently mentioned is the famous scandal caused by the book and the resulting sales of over three hundred thousand copies.

As accomplishments in the author's career, these facts deserve perpetuating but certainly not at the cost of forgetting numerous matters of greater importance. For instance, these historians have failed to note her artistic development from sentimental romancer for popular magazines to an accomplished novelist; her chronicling of, and comments upon, many social issues of the eras in which she lived and worked; her female protagonist who dominates virtually all her plots and who reflects the feministic convictions of her creator; and finally the historical importance of her life itself, both in terms of ancestry and of professional and social relationships.

Such facts have most probably been neglected because the acme of the Princess' career, reflected in *World's-End* (1914) and *Shadows of Flames* (1915)—and duly noted by contemporary reviewers—was followed by a world war, then by a slowing in her literary production (1920–30), and ultimately by virtual silence from 1930 until her death in 1945. Writers of her obituary notices remembered only that she was the author "of best sellers in the nineties."

This book, the first one ever published about Princess Troubetzkoy, has grown from the conviction that her life and her artistic achievements are worthy both of historical record and of critical treatment. The primary aim of this study is to present in a single volume the historical, biographical, and critical information necessary for tracing the major developments of her life and for giving a well-balanced view of her work. Because there is an unusually close correlation between her life and her work, and because the best biographical information is either unpublished or generally inaccessible, the volume has a biographical emphasis; it is not, properly speaking, a "biography." Material concerning the author's life has been greatly condensed and presented primarily as an aid to understanding the genesis and content of the two dozen books, all of which are discussed.

The study does not, however, pretend to be exhaustive even in the area of criticism. Numerous titles invite treatment from several approaches, but only the mode or modes suggested by the most salient aspects of the various works have been employed. Quite obviously, therefore, there is much left to be said from many critical perspectives.

Because the primary theme is the development of the artist and because the line of development shows, on balance, increasing maturity (although with several regressions), the basic organizational principle has been chronological. The chronological pattern has been set forth not only by dividing the material into five convenient chapter divisions but also by designating two distinct artistic periods—the first, or experimental, period beginning in 1886 with the publication of "A Brother to Dragons" and ending in 1898 with the romance *A Damsel Errant;* the second, or mature, period beginning in 1905 with *Seléné,* a poem in the Esthete mode, and extending through the performance of *The Young Elizabeth* in 1938.

Chapter 1 discusses various formative influences and ends with a discussion of "A Brother to Dragons" (1886), the story which, showing the effect of these forces, began her literary career. Her marriage to John Armstrong Chanler and her artistic progress, shown later in the 1880's, are discussed in Chapter 2. This advance is paralleled by a turn to Realistic setting and characters.

Chapter 3 treats her first marriage also, her association with the "Souls" of London, and analyzes *Barbara Dering* (1892), the finest work of the first period. The beginning of the second period —her divorce and her marriage to Prince Pierre Troubetzkoy—

Preface

is discussed in Chapter 4. *Seléné* and *Augustine the Man,* a closet drama, point toward the Realistic novels *World's-End* (1914) and *Shadows of Flames* (1915), discussed in Chapter 5, which concerns the years 1908–45—the more important artistic period. Chapter 6 summarizes the various accomplishments set forth in the first five chapters, as well as the most fundamental weaknesses of the works.

Because Princess Troubetzkoy ordered that her private papers be destroyed at her death, only a few escaped, and these are scattered to the farthest extremities of the United States. I am therefore grateful to a number of libraries for permission to study these collections and for cooperation in obtaining photocopies. Among the most helpful were the University of Virginia, University of Texas, Duke University, the Virginia Historical Society, the Virginia State Library, and the Enoch Pratt Library. For more general help, I am indebted to Colonel and Mrs. Clarke Lawrence and to various staff members of the British Museum and of the United States Information Service in Milan. I am also indebted to my colleagues at the University of Richmond, especially Dr. Gene Adrean and Mr. Guy St. Clair, who were most generous with both their time and their highly specialized knowledge.

Numerous individuals kindly helped supply information for which there are no printed or manuscript sources. Of these, I am most especially grateful to Mr. and Mrs. Allen Potts, Mr. Edmund Archer, Mr. and Mrs. Alexander Rives, Mr. Hoskins Mallory Sclater, and Mrs. Robert Page, all kinsmen of the Princess, who gave and never counted the cost. I am also indebted to the Principessa Mary Troubetzkoy and to the staff members of the Troubetzkoy Museum at Pallanza for bringing to life the atmosphere of their lovely region which the Princess had written about almost seventy years before my visits there in 1967 and in 1971. Finally, I am grateful to my wife, Carole Wickham Taylor, who has patiently endured the many problems I have encountered, has read my manuscript and made helpful suggestions, and has helped immeasurably to make the final preparations for publication. I mention her name last in order that it receive emphasis over all others.

W. D. T.

The University of Richmond

Acknowledgments

In addition to those cited in the preface for their help in gathering various materials, I am indebted to the following persons and institutions:

The manuscript staff of the Alderman Library of the University of Virginia for their aid in obtaining permissions to quote, especially to Mr. Edmund Berkley and Mrs. Anne Freudenberg.

Mr. Frank Morley and Mr. MacDonald Wellford for granting the above permissions.

The Harvard College Library for permission to quote from their collection of Troubetzkoy letters.

The Duke University Library for permission to quote from the John Armstrong Chaloner papers.

The Virginia Historical Society for permission to quote from the Rives papers and from *The Virginia Magazine of History and Biography*.

Mr. Edmund Archer for permission to quote from personal interviews and from a letter written by Princess Troubetzkoy to his mother, Mrs. Rosalie Pleasants Archer.

The University of Richmond Committee on Faculty Research for two grants which helped defray a portion of the cost of preparing this volume.

Contents

Chronology

1863 Amélie Louise Rives born in Richmond, Virginia, the first child of Confederate Colonel and Mrs. Alfred Landon Rives; soon taken to Castle Hill, the Rives ancestral home in Albemarle County.

1870 Studied music and drawing in Mobile; studied under governesses and tutors for next several years.

1886 Published "A Brother to Dragons" (short story) in *Atlantic Monthly*.

1887 Continued to publish in popular magazines; first season in Newport; met John Armstrong Chanler, great-grandson of John Jacob Astor.

1888 "Virginia of Virginia" (first piece of extended fiction); *Herod and Mariamne* (first drama); *The Quick or the Dead?* (first novel) sold three hundred thousand copies and caused furor; married John Armstrong Chanler on June 15.

1889 *Witness of the Sun* (first novel with European setting); visited England; entertained by George Curzon and the "Souls"; studied art in Paris.

1890 Chanler started "Paris Prize Fund"; marital rift began.

1891 Amélie Rives returned to the United States; continued art study.

1892 *Barbara Dering*, sequel to *The Quick or the Dead?* and the finest work of the first period (1886–98).

1893 *Tanis, the Sang-Digger.*

1894 Separation from Chanler; introduced in London by Oscar Wilde to Prince Pierre Troubetzkoy; visited Prince's family on the Lago Maggiore.

1895 Divorced from Chanler.

1896 Married Russian Prince Pierre Troubetzkoy on February 27.

1898 Ended first artistic period with *A Damsel Errant.*
1905 Began second artistic period with *Seléné,* a narrative poem in the Esthete mode.
1906 *Augustine the Man.*
1908 *The Golden Rose,* her finest Romantic novel.
1910 *Pan's Mountain.*
1912 *Hidden House,* first ghost story.
1914 *World's-End* (Realistic novel); visited Europe for the last time.
1915 *Shadows of Flames.*
1916– Broadway successes: *The Fear Market* (motion picture
1920 version, 1920); *Allegiance; The Prince and the Pauper.*
1924 *The Sea-Woman's Cloak,* presented by Richard Boleslawsky's Laboratory Theatre.
1926 *The Queerness of Celia.*
1930 *Firedamp,* final book.
1936 Prince Troubetzkoy died August 25.
1938 *The Young Elizabeth,* presented by St. Louis Little Theatre.
1945 Princess Troubetzkoy died August 16.

Amélie Rives
(Princess Troubetzkoy)

CHAPTER *1*

Early Life: 1863–86

CASTLE HILL, the seat of the Rives family of Virginia, is situated among that spur of Blue Ridge foothills commonly called the "Southwest Range" or "Western Mountains." The mansion fits well into the architectural fabric of the region (the central town of which is Charlottesville): its western wing is a late Colonial clapboard structure with tall dormers; the eastern wing, which backs upon it, is Federal and is faced with Roman columns. Running eastward from this wing is a lawn shaped like an hourglass; its boundaries are outlined by solid walls of boxwood, which are said to be the tallest in Virginia and well over two hundred years old.

Colonial houses, Federal houses, and boxwood are symbolic both of this area and also of most of eastern Virginia. But Castle Hill suggests a more specific symbolism: the Colonial wing stands as an unofficial memorial to its builder, Dr. Thomas Walker, the pioneer physician who entered Kentucky in 1750, preceding Daniel Boone by some twenty years. The Federal wing recalls William Cabell Rives—orator, United States senator, and twice minister plenipotentiary to France—who built it in the early nineteenth century shortly after his marriage to Judith Page Walker, Dr. Walker's granddaughter.

In the long life of the house of more than two centuries, Castle Hill has counted among its guests six presidents of the United States; such foreign dignitaries as the Marquis de Lafayette and George Curzon; literary figures ranging from Ellen Glasgow to H. L. Mencken and from Joseph Hergesheimer to Thomas Nelson Page; and colorful historical figures like Jack Jouett and General Tarleton, who stopped within hours of each other on their famous race to Monticello. Its rooms have contained exquisite French Empire pieces; its walls, portraits by L. M. D. Guillaume and charcoals by Saint-Mémin. Its stables have boasted such stallions as Arnon; its hunting pack has achieved national recognition.

Such facts have long been the fascination of Virginia historians, and they contain definite intrinsic interest.[1] More important, though, are the ways in which they shaped the life and art of Amélie Rives. Castle Hill figures prominently in approximately half of her published works, and its indirect influence can be traced in most of the others. Her career spanned forty-four years; her work ranged from the highly fanciful to the sharply Realistic; but, in it, Castle Hill remains ever the same. Quite often it is thinly disguised as the setting for a novel; sometimes it is used in just a few scenes; but it always functions the same way: as an objective correlative conveying a feeling of permanence and stability in the midst of a changing American society which to the author was anything but permanent and stable. From the family documents which have survived, it is possible to trace this influence fairly thoroughly.

I Heritage and Education

Amélie Louise Rives was born on August 23, 1863, in the old rectory of St. Paul's Episcopal Church in Richmond. At this time, as throughout the Civil War, her father, Alfred Landon Rives, served as Colonel of Engineers on the staff of General Robert E. Lee, who was to become her godfather. She was the first child of Colonel and Mrs. Rives (the former Sarah Catherine Macmurdo); and both parents, along with her paternal grandmother, Judith Page Rives, selected her name after long deliberation. The first wife of King Louis Philippe had been named Amélie, and she and Judith Page Rives had been intimate friends during William Cabell Rives's first ministry to France. Queen Amélie had been godmother to the Rives's daughter born during this ministry, and they had named her for the queen. This sister of Colonel Rives became a popular Virginia belle in her teens and married Henry Sigourney of Boston in 1854. In 1873, she, her husband, and three of their children foundered on the French SS *Ville du Havre,* en route to Paris.[2]

As soon as the conditions of Civil War and Sarah Rives's health permitted, the infant Amélie Rives and her mother were taken to Castle Hill to join Colonel Rives's parents. There, they resided safely for the remainder of the war. Though Judith Page Rives expressed fear that "the sad and terrible changes wrought by wicked men" [3] might destroy her home and her family, and though the fighting came within a few miles, the plantation escaped untouched.

Senator and Mrs. William Cabell Rives took an active interest in their granddaughter's rearing and education. To this task they brought the experience of many years in the French court and among intellectual circles in Washington and Richmond, not to mention their own educations which had been obtained from the best tutors available in the Commonwealth of Virginia. More importantly, both were literary people; Senator Rives was the author of a biography of James Madison and Judith Page Rives of two autobiographical volumes about her residence in Europe.[4] As Amélie was an exceptionally bright child, her education began early. At four, she learned to read; by six, she could read well enough "to enjoy Hans Andersen fairy tales and to ask for the real Shakespeare instead of 'Lamb's Tales from Shakespeare.'" [5] Just how early she began to write is unknown, but she began to do so at a time when she was unable to distinguish capital from lower-case letters. In 1925, while reminiscing to a friend about her early education, she related an anecdote which well illustrates her natural inclination to write. When she was about ten, she filled so much paper with her childish poems and dramas that her mother thought her wasteful and refused to give her more. So she turned to the next most logical place: the five-inch hem of her white, starched petticoat. Her father, learning of the incident, said that she was to have all the paper she wanted.[6]

In true humanistic fashion, her education was extended to other areas besides belles-lettres. Just after the Civil War, Colonel Rives took the position of chief superintendent and general manager of the Mobile and Ohio Railway; and, during the winters which the family spent with him in Mobile, Amélie studied music under a "Miss Evy," who ran a private school in the city, and "academic drawing" at the Mobile Academy of Design. But, for the most part, her education was privately directed by tutors and governesses, as her father distrusted private schools. Language study was also begun very early, and special emphasis was given to Latin and to French, which was often spoken in the household.

Physical exercise was also part of the curriculum; and horseback riding, which she began at the age of four, was always one of her favorite recreations.

The names of these tutors and governesses are forgotten. There is every indication, however, that they used wise judgment in the education of their charge. Several of Amélie's drawings, done in her early teens, show a fine sense of proportion and line. Interesting, too, is the fact that she correlated her various studies very skillfully. Frequently a page would contain a series of drawings with an accompanying narrative or a set of captions. Also, several of her early watercolors exist,[7] and one in particular shows especially well her developing artistic sense. It is contained in a book of color illustrations faced by drawings of the same scenes. The student was directed to paint the drawings as nearly like the original as he could. The scene in question shows two mothers watching their children at play. All are standing in a hayfield during a harvest; the field is surrounded by trees in autumn foliage. The colors of the original are well coordinated, with careful attention paid to the coloring of small details. Amélie's version, while using primary colors, is much cleverer than the original in that she has played down much of the unimportant detail and focused attention on the bright clothing of the boy and girl. Thus was exhibited a developing sense of proportion and a clear, straightforward emphasis upon important details—the characteristics of all she ever wrote.

The influence of the tutors and governesses was fortunately supplemented by that of parents and grandparents. Amélie was given free reign of Senator Rives's library (which numbered several thousand volumes); and she read, as her interest dictated, a truly eclectic assortment of them. These ranged from *The Letters of Junius* to the *Nibelungenlied;* from illustrated volumes of the naturalist Georges Louis Buffon to the medieval chronicles of Jean Froissart; from the Robin Hood legends (on which she wrote an early drama) to Shakespeare and numerous other Elizabethan and Jacobean dramatists, whose language infuses her earliest published stories.

Concurrent with this program of formal (if somewhat permissive) education, the more subtle development of tastes and social attitudes was also occurring. The tastes can be rather easily summarized: being descended from two aristocratic families, most of whose associations were among people of their own class and background, young Amélie soon developed sophisticated tastes in the creative and decorative arts and in dress, speech, and manners. These traits she never compromised, even in later life when her income was at times sharply curbed. After her marriage to Prince Pierre Troubetzkoy, she was commonly referred to as "The Princess," a title which seemed as natural for her as it seemed fitting to those who used it.

The social attitudes which Amélie was forming during this period are more difficult to describe, for they are more complex than the matter of taste. Taste, of course, is a private matter; and, in exercising it, one normally has to answer only to his private esthetic conscience. Social attitudes are different; with them, the feelings and well-being of others are involved and must be considered. In the most consistent of people, however, such attitudes are often inconsistent. The influences which shaped the young Amélie's social conscience were both varied and inconsistent; but, once fixed, their effect was unchanging and long lasting. The basic tenet in her social credo was a traditional aristocratic belief in a stratified society. From a very early age she lived with the awareness of her aristocratic Virginia heritage—an awareness that was in no sense provincial; it simply meant that, in the Reconstruction South, the only place for the exchange of ideas or for intellectual companionship was among similar people of privilege, and this environment was the only one in which she felt at home. The one common denominator among her tastes, her social outlook, and her art was quality. The commonplace and the vulgar both bored and repulsed her. This reaction was no affectation: such was her nature.

This selectivity does not mean, though, that she accepted the position into which birth had placed her with an attitude which in any way resembled snobbery. On the contrary, she felt that she and all others favored by privilege inherited with their positions the responsibility to care for or about the less fortunate. She adhered to this idea in theory as well as in practice. It was common for critics to proclaim her lower characters as being among her best; and such praise was well justified, for these creations were always portrayed sympathetically and with brilliant perception. Even her first published story, "A Brother to Dragons," for all its structural and stylistic weakness, is saved in some measure by the

point of view of the earthy servant Anthony Butter. Also, a large
part of the royalties from *The Quick or the Dead?* was used to
help the plight of poor Negroes in Albemarle County, and records
of her attempts to help improve labor conditions are frequent.

Such social concepts, if not in vogue in the present day, were
scarcely original with the young woman. One can easily compare
them to the principles of Jeffersonian democracy, which they parallel rather closely. Their chief source is immediately obvious, as
Senator Rives is often called "the political child" of his close friend
and neighbor Thomas Jefferson. Regarded in this light, her spectrum of social ideas, which embraced the aristocratic concept of
social privilege at one pole and a compassionate concern for all
levels of humanity at the other, appears quite consistent. Even her
concept of God was much like Jefferson's. Her deity was, quite
simply, a combination of love and wisdom; and she served Him
dutifully.

By her late teens, Amélie had developed distinctive physical
features to accompany her strong ideas. Her regal bearing gave
the impression of height, but she was in reality rather short. She
frequently wore long, flowing gowns to add height and grace to a
figure of disproportionately short legs and long waist. A steel engraving which accompanied the first edition of *The Quick or the
Dead?*, her most famous novel, reveals large sensitive eyes, an
aquiline nose, and a profusion of ash-blonde hair. All photographs
(she was probably the most photographed Virginian of the nineteenth century) show a stateliness of carriage and an aura of
nobility. Her face revealed a capacity for kindness as well as a
characteristic dignity. Even the most grudging of critics were
forced to speak of her as a person in superlatives, and no commentator seemed able to take her lightly.

It is important to view these brief physical characteristics along
with her social ideas. Although her ideas found their way into
fiction, as would be expected, it is unusual that her physical characteristics did also. Most of her stories concern a young woman,
usually with blonde hair, who is quite vivacious. She cuts a daring
figure through a series of adventures and usually dominates the
action; but she always possesses a compassionate side and is willing to make unlimited sacrifices for the good of others. The beauty
of young Amélie and her social attitudes both indicate a strong
sense of security. It is only natural to assume that such security

promotes an assertion of the ego, and she asserted hers. That she channeled this assertion in the direction of literature has proved the gain of posterity.

II   *A Sister to Dragons: 1886–88*

As is understandable with prodigies reared in an adult atmosphere, Amélie's mind matured quickly, and most of the opinions and attitudes already described were apparently formed by her late teens. And all the while she was writing. Only fragments of this juvenilia exist today, and it is perhaps just as well. Until 1886, when she was twenty-three, she wrote only for personal enjoyment; and her efforts were seen by no one outside the family. Judging from her first published story and from mention of an early Robin Hood drama (which has not survived), one concludes that these productions stemmed from her reading of Elizabethan plays and medieval legends such as those described above. Because her fiction was not intended for publication, there was little consideration given to who potential readers might be or on what level they might comprehend. Had she continued to write only for her own pleasure, her approach might have continued blissfully innocent; and she would have been personally none the worse for it.

However, in 1885 this situation suddenly changed, and she was wrenched from the world of the naïve amateur and thrust into the public arena of professionalism. In the late summer of 1885, William Sigourney Otis, a family friend from Boston, was visiting Castle Hill. While going through some of Sarah Rives's music in the drawing room, he found the manuscript of the story "A Brother to Dragons"; and, learning that Amélie was the author, he asked her permission to take it with him to Boston. After making him promise that he would not reveal who had written it, she consented; and the manuscript soon found its way into the hands of Thomas Bailey Aldrich, editor of the *Atlantic Monthly*. Aldrich was enthusiastic; and, after getting the author's name from Otis, he immediately sent Amélie a laudatory letter. This gesture began an enthusiastic exchange of correspondence between the two, which had slowed markedly by March, 1886, when "A Brother to Dragons" finally saw print in the *Atlantic Monthly*. By then, Aldrich had become critical of her work, having seen manuscripts of some subsequent stories. Amélie, who smarted from these judgments, ended the exchange with a cold letter which expressed regret over the fact that he did not think her work was progressing.[8] Thus, her first relationship with a publisher came to an unhappy end.

But demanding editors like Aldrich were not the sole arbiters of taste in the 1880's, and "A Brother to Dragons" enjoyed an enthusiastic reception. Set in the Warwickshire of "Master Shakespeare," the story was written in Elizabethan idiom and was narrated by a servant named Anthony Butter. Butter, like the many low characters who descend from him in Amélie's stories, novels, and dramas, is one of the sharpest drawn characters in the story.

The protagonist of the tale, Lady Margaret of Amhurste, controls the action throughout. After scaring her brother, Lord Robert, by dressing as a ghost, she weeps bitterly when he leaves their ancestral home, much humiliated by the incident. Three years later, she, an attractive and eligible young maiden, is sought by many suitors; but none pleases her. She is interested only in Lord Denbeigh, a reputed rake who lives nearby. What others regard as evil in the young nobleman, her charitable heart tells her is simply misfortune. But he, recognizing her goodness and seeing his own indiscretions in their true light, feels incapable of escaping his former life.

Moreover, he is involved in some sort of intrigue (one never explained). Lady Margaret, who finds out about the intrigue (by unexplained means), sends Butter to protect him. Butter sees the long-absent Robert return and beg Lord Denbeigh not to hold a rendezvous he has planned for two nights hence in London. Upon telling Lady Margaret the news, Butter is dispatched to London where, in the altercation that ensues, he sees Lord Robert stabbed while trying to protect Lord Denbeigh from an assailant. As Lord Denbeigh undresses Lord Robert to care for his wound, he suddenly gives a strange cry: the victim is not Lord Robert but Lady Margaret in disguise (a favorite Shakespearean device). While all male heads are turned, her wounds are bound. They heal, of course, in time for her and the now repentant Lord Denbeigh to exchange expressions of love. Just after this episode, Denbeigh sails with Essex to Spain, where he has heard Lord Robert is held prisoner. Lord Robert returns with him, but Denbeigh has re-

ceived severe wounds. These soon heal, and he and Lady Margaret are married shortly thereafter.

In a sort of coda (its relationship to the main story is never
established), Lord Denbeigh is summoned to fight for the queen.
Lord Robert, who is visiting Lord and Lady Denbeigh, goes in his
stead to leave Lord Denbeigh near his wife when their first child
is born. Their happiness is tempered, however, by the news of
Lord Robert's death in the wars. The story ends with Lady Margaret drawing Lord Denbeigh and the child to her breast.

With its setting in a far-off land and time, "A Brother to Dragons" pleased the average reader of the mass American audience—
one comprised of what Lizette Woodworth Reese has called "a
romantic, poorly educated woman . . . who at that time filled
the position now held by the average female frequenter of the
movies." [9] Earlier in the 1880's this reader's taste had been satisfied by such romances as Lew Wallace's *Ben-Hur* (1880) and
Robert Louis Stevenson's *Prince Otto* (1885). In the following
decade Anthony Hope's *Prisoner of Zenda* (1894) and Henryk
Sienkiewicz's *Quo Vadis?* (1896) fulfilled the same taste.[10]

Readers who thrilled to the thundering of Ben-Hur's chariot
were concerned primarily with the romantic dreams suggested by
such stories, and they either ignored or overlooked technical
flaws. Subsequent critics—present-day ones, in particular—have
not been kind to the popular works of this period; for modern
critics have a pronounced tendency to exalt the Realistic, sometimes in extreme forms, and to degrade the Romantic. It is not
likely, therefore, that they would take kindly to an age which ran
sales of sentimental romances like *Quo Vadis?* into the hundreds
of thousands and which left the volumes of William Dean Howells and Henry James to gather dust on the shelves of any book-
seller daring enough to stock them. On the other hand, there are
sufficient objective reasons why this literature is for the most part
ignored by serious critics; and most of these are reflected in "A
Brother to Dragons."

In the story, as in the age, the prevailing attitude was one of
idealization: life is viewed as if through the famous rose-colored
glasses. Love is an emotion of the nobility, experienced as a reward to heroism. Death is a noble incident on the field of battle.
Lord Robert and Lord Denbeigh are flat creations who perform

such stock acts as fighting in foreign wars and getting involved in vague espionage intrigues, and their feelings or thoughts are never revealed.

Equally glaring is a weakness of plot structure. Instead of the logical chain of cause-effect factors which characterizes the organic evolution of the well-made plot, one finds simply a series of events tacked together in unmotivated chronology and pointing to no logical resolution. The coda, for instance, seems an arbitrary afterthought. Its apparent purpose is merely to add a note of tragedy to the happily resolved love story of Lady Margaret and Lord Denbeigh. One can, of course, appreciate the attempt to end the story in a manner other than the happy-ever-after formula, but the contrived death of the hero is hardly a satisfactory alternative, since it undermines an already creaking plot structure.

Other defects are found in the author's faltering control of certain scenes and occasionally in her language. For instance, in the serious scene near the end in which Lady Margaret has fainted and Lord Robert is ready to sacrifice his life for Lord Denbeigh, there is an interruptive burlesque scene in which Butter collides with Lord Robert. Just after Lord Denbeigh's London rendezvous, he starts to follow his wounded friend, whom he thinks to be Lord Robert. In so doing, Denbeigh leaves behind a friend who has accompanied him on the mission "to swallow the moonshine with his great gaping mouth." [11] The ridiculousness of this scene is surpassed only by the metaphor used to express it, a figure which indicates the overly exuberant language of many passages. An even better example is found in Butter's description of Lady Margaret's actions after scaring her brother with her ghost disguise: "With mine own eyes I saw her, on the day he set forth, cling to his neck, and when he shook her thence, hang about his loins, and when at last he pushed her to the ground, she laid her hands about his feet and wept; and between every sob it was, 'Go not, brother, for my fault! . . .' " (291).

Such instances of naïve effusiveness are found in several places in the story, but they are not frequent enough to mar the style as a whole. As a matter of fact, the general effect of the author's improvised Elizabethan dialect has a rather true ring. Nevertheless, various critics complained that Amélie did not follow linguistic law to the letter. Lacking the discipline of either a semanticist or a philologist, such would have been impossible for her; moreover, linguistic purity was not her intention in the first place. Rather, she was attempting to create an impression of a particular time and place by means of language, and she was able to do so by following the spirit of the linguistic law and not its letter. Regarded in this light, the language of the Elizabethans in this initial story compares rather favorably with the mountaineer twang and the Gaelic brogue in later stories and dramas, which critics were to admire.

III   *The Birth of a Heroine*

Although "A Brother to Dragons" could never be called a distinguished performance, it contains one distinct foreshadowing of better things to come: the protagonist, Lady Margaret. Though she may physically resemble the traditional blonde heroine of popular romance, the similarity ends there. Instead of being weak and retiring like these prototypes, her outstanding characteristics are robustness, vivaciousness, and strength of character. These qualities appear again and again in Amélie's future work, for the majority of her subsequent works center around a strong female protagonist. A full-scale view of this work reveals that, whatever the time or place in which a plot is set, the heroine is but an extension of, and variation upon, Lady Margaret; most often, such a protagonist wears more modern clothes and speaks in contemporary idiom, but she faces vicissitudes which would destroy the stock sentimental heroine.

Moreover, there is always an aura of plenitude about her: she is not merely pretty, but beautiful; not merely active, but often athletic and competitive in matters of physical ability. Her hair is the most outstanding aspect of her beauty, and it invariably cascades in great profusion down her back. She has a capacity for love, but never for the restrained conventional variety; rather, hers is a love of the soul which includes all natural beings. When the love object is a particular man, such affection embraces him completely and makes no compromises short of complete spiritual oneness.

As with the characters of Henry James, this heroine is seldom concerned with mundane circumstances such as earning a living. Rather, she is faced with some sort of major emotional crisis. In the later fiction of Amélie, she gradually grows older and somewhat sadder and wiser, having been tempered by unhappiness in love, by war, or by exploitation of her trusting nature. Still she walks through the pages of Amélie's work resolute and unafraid.

Those who saw Amélie's heroine only in "A Brother to Dragons" and in the Elizabethan stories which immediately followed [12] might have attributed both her own genesis and that of the plots in which she appeared to Shakespeare. It is true that the device of the strong female dominating the action of the plot and controlling its direction was a Shakespearean favorite, as witnessed by Portia in *The Merchant of Venice* and by Viola in *Twelfth Night*. But to those who followed the evolution of Amélie's heroine through *Firedamp* (1930), the last published work, and who kept abreast of the much publicized events of the author's career, it was obvious that this protagonist was first and foremost an extension of her creator in both physique and character; and her adventures were frequently those of the author, thinly disguised. To trace the course of Amélie Rives's career, then, is to study the correlation of her life to her work and to center the discussion of the latter upon this dynasty of heroines.

CHAPTER *2*

From Romance to Realism: 1886–88

WITH minor variations, the stories which appeared between "A Brother to Dragons" and "Virginia of Virginia" (January, 1888) represent an extension of the original vein. Two more[1] are set in Elizabethan and Jacobean England and are narrated in the idiom of the period. One[2] is set just before Noah's flood and one[3] in ancient Greece; but these changes indicate only that the author's fancy had changed location. The weaknesses of the first story are continued; and, assuming that Aldrich had had one of these stories in mind when he remarked that its author had not progressed from her first effort, he was certainly correct. Nevertheless, it was as a writer of national fame that Amélie accompanied her mother to Newport in the summer of 1887 for her first season. There, as a guest of her uncle, William C. Rives, she became one of the most discussed debutantes of the year.

Sometime during this summer, while attending a dinner party given by a Mrs. King, she met John Armstrong Chanler, a great-grandson of John Jacob Astor and a grandson of Sam Ward. Chanler was the social and, to some degree, the intellectual equal of Amélie; for his father, a Columbia University professor, had sent him to Rugby, Columbia, the Collège de France, and the Ecole des Sciences Politiques. Chanler, now established as an attorney and enjoying himself by cutting a grand social figure among the elite circles of New York and Newport, immediately fell in love with the famous young lady from Virginia. During September and the Christmas holidays of 1887, he visited Castle Hill, where he apparently pressed his suit very hard; and, during still another visit he was finally accepted by Amélie as her future husband in April, 1888.

I *"Virginia of Virginia"* (*1888*)

The pleasant experiences of 1887 might well have caused Amélie to write of white-clad debutantes flanked by the moonlit
waters of Newport, or of dashing beaux and of the happy-ever-
after. Instead, her next story concerned a girl of rural Virginia
whose only social graces were an ability to play simple melodies
on the piano and a slight knowledge of the English Cavalier
poets. Instead of the expected emphasis on manners and dress,
there is rather an interest in strength of character, as shown in the
heroine's simple honesty, self-sacrifice, and loyalty to the man she
loves. In short, the story shows that Amélie's successful debut and
the attentions of a highly desirable bachelor had little affected her
secure sense of identity. That she delighted in recent events there
can be no question; but, instead of having them turn her head to
the fripperies of the debutante's life, her character was strong
enough to assimilate them. Though the love theme in the new
story is obviously based upon the author's newly gained knowledge of the subject, it is a natural kind of love, one free from the
artifices of the gallant suitor and the breathless virgin. New experience was teaching her to see more deeply into the life of things.

"Virginia of Virginia" is set in the author's native Albemarle
County at Caryston, a plantation closely resembling Castle Hill.
The analogous heroine is Virginia Herrick, daughter of the earthy
plantation manager. When a young Englishman named Jack
Roden buys Caryston as a horse-breeding farm, he is helped in his
new venture by Virginia's father, who becomes overseer, and by
Virginia herself, who acts as cook and housekeeper. Though
Roden is impressed by Virginia's beauty and by her fine singing
voice, the affection that grows between the two is largely Virginia's. Though usually plain-spoken, she cannot stoop to let her
feelings be known. Even though she saves Roden's life after a
riding accident, he is still rather reserved in his feelings for her.
He thinks of her as a friend rather than as a possible wife, and his
coolness eventually causes him to confide to her that he is engaged
to Mary Erroll, a cultivated young lady who lives close by.

With her usual honesty, Virginia tries to accept this fact; but
she backslides at a most inopportune time by giving Roden's intended a dress to wear which she believes to be contaminated

with fever germs. When Mary falls ill of the fever, Virginia, prodded by her conscience, nurses her back to health and almost kills herself in doing so. Of course, she has to tell Roden of her wrongdoing. Without forgiving her, he leaves on a holiday; and, while he is away, his barn catches on fire. Hoping to atone for her sin, Virginia rushes in the burning building and saves Bonnibel, Roden's prize mount; but she is knocked unconscious by a falling beam before she can get out. As she dies with her father and Roden by her side, she deliriously expresses her love for the Englishman.

Aside from the final scene, which borders on the melodramatic, and a few additional flaws, "Virginia of Virginia" was a decisive step forward in the artistic development of Amélie Rives. It was a longer story than any she had written, and she seemed to profit from the extra length by unfolding her plot more gradually and by developing character and incident more fully than before. Virginia Herrick is first seen as the young daughter of a poor farmer, then as a young woman in love for the first time, and subsequently as a jilted lover unafraid to take her destiny into her own hands.

Though the length of "Virginia of Virginia" places it in that no-man's-land between what is definitely called novel or definitely a short story, thus making its genre debatable,[4] it is sufficiently longer than anything Amélie had formerly written to indicate that her talents were best suited for more extended narratives. It is significant that most of her subsequent efforts were either lengthy stories or novels. There is, however, a definite limit to the advantages offered by mere length. But, short or long, "Virginia of Virginia" would be seen as a clear improvement over the earlier stories. The major reason is the Realism, sorely lacking before but found in numerous manifestations here.

Though Realism and Sentimentality are matters of taste and are not normally bases for evaluating the success of a work of art, it is obvious that much of this story's strength lies in its Realistic elements. The view of life is, on the whole, sharper than before, as is the concept of the causative forces which shape the destinies of the characters. Virginia Herrick's actions are far better understood than were, say, those of Lady Margaret in "A Brother to Dragons." For instance, there is an easily traceable chain of events which ultimately causes Virginia's death: she falls in love, is rejected, jealously tries to destroy her rival, almost succceeds, then repents and dies in the attempt. Also, for the first time, there is something like a complete milieu presented. Two social levels—the aristocracy and the yeomanry—provide a believable social context; and the author is obviously aware how both strata think and talk. Virginia, for instance, intrudes a "y" into words beginning with palatal stops, making "garden" "gyarden"; "card" "cyard," just as natives of her region did in real life. Her father is the man of the soil personified; and he also has an appropriate accent and an uncomplicated sense of right and wrong, like his daughter.

This story, then, was cut not from a standard bolt of literary commonplaces but from one of the author's own weaving. It shows that she had come to realize the fictional potential offered by her own time and place, as well as her ability to mold her observations of the present into meaningful form. It is not surprising that Virginia Herrick, who closely resembles her originator both emotionally and physically, should stand out as the most salient of these details. "Virginia of Virginia" is important if only because it is the author's first of many subsequent attempts at treating a modern heroine and setting.

Most critics agreed that "Virginia of Virginia" outshone all former stores and that its Realism was vivid. The English critic Hamilton Aïdé went so far as to say that it impressed him as being "a transcript direct from nature." [5] Yet Aïdé and others noticed an unfinished quality which was especially obvious in certain unconventional expressions. Aïdé astutely sensed that these were the result of writing at "white heat" and that they could have been corrected by careful revision. Yet, he was the first to admit that, in Amélie's case, there was more to be gained than lost by hasty composition; for composing while inspiration was fresh gave the writing a freshness which revision might have dulled. This judgment was as sound as it was prophetic; for there is only one existing manuscript[6] which shows any significant revision, and future published works were to strike reviewers as highly original, if not always polished.

In the light of modern criticism, one sees both "Virginia of Virginia" and all of Amélie's work preceding 1898 as productions of a mind molded by a variety of influences but not controlled by any one of them. The language is something unique, being the blend of poetic phrases and antiquated idioms juxtaposed against a natural and somewhat naïve exuberance. Smoke rises in an "ever ascending spiral"(212); an advantageous position is an archaic "coign of vantage"(195); one o'clock in the afternoon is "one of the clock"(200). And, though one reviewer warned that such idiosyncrasies were rather "too like Mr. [Edgar] Saltus's obelisk, which was arrestive and his labyrinth, which was incircuitable," [7] the style found disfavor only among the purists, whose eagerness to find minor faults obscured the overriding fact that "Virginia of Virginia" represented Amélie's decided progress in the more important areas of plotting, characterization, and Realism.

II The Quick or the Dead? (1888)

Doubtlessly heartened by the favorable reviews of "Virginia of Virginia," Amélie Rives spent the late winter months of 1888 entertaining the courtship of John Armstrong Chanler and preparing her first novel for publication. Both the book and Chanler's courtship would have a strong bearing on each other, and both were to change not only her life but also the course of her career. April proved eventually to have been the cruelest of months for both Chanler and Amélie, but at the moment Chanler had won the girl he had been courting for nine months, and *The Quick or the Dead?* led off the April issue of *Lippincott's Monthly Magazine*, faced by a fine engraving of the author.

The engraving was appropriately placed, as *The Quick or the Dead?* featured another heroine who closely resembled Amélie. She can perhaps best be described as an extremely refined and sophisticated version of Virginia Herrick. But, whereas Virginia had been concerned with the problem of winning and keeping the man she loved, Barbara Pomfret, the new protagonist, is caught in the dilemma of whether to remain true to the memory of her departed husband or to marry his cousin. This problem furnishes the novel with both its title and its plot.

Barbara is first seen returning to Rosemary, the plantation where she had lived with her husband Valentine, now dead for several months. Though she is at first dominated by the sentimental urge to try to recapture the past by touching things he had owned, she gradually gains a certain emotional equilibrium; and she eventually becomes "mistress of a rare art, that of controlling her thoughts. . . ." [8] Soon Jock Dering, Val's cousin, arrives on the scene, and each likes the other. Though they get on well, she is

troubled from the first by his resemblance to Val—one so striking
that at times she believes him to be his cousin reincarnate; and she
fights against this sentimental morbidity.

One day, when she chances to notice the blue veins on her fore-
arm, she remembers that Val used to kiss her there and falls into a
fit of weeping. She is able to keep these feelings repressed until
one afternoon when she and Jock are caught in a thunderstorm (a frequent occurrence in Amélie's love stories). The rising
passion of the storm strips away inhibition long enough for each
to acknowledge an intellectual sympathy with the other. When
Barbara utters "How alike we are!," the author intrudes (as she
seldom does) to explain that "This sentence always marks a distinct epoch in the acquaintance of a man and woman. The hands
of friendship are drawn apart as by two passing trains, and
friendship is left on the siding . . ."(453).

This scene proves to be the motivating incident: the seed of
love has been sown, and its erratic growth forms the major action.
When Jock learns of her groundless concern about his resemblance to Val, he tries to bring her to reason. He succeeds until
she finds that he carries a picture of Val about with him, for this
discovery causes a relapse. Though he tells her of his determina-
tion to conquer her fears and to win her entirely for himself, she
answers, "There is a grave between us—there is an open grave
between us" (466); and she becomes adamant to his arguments.

He leaves for New York, and she seems confirmed in having let
him go after visiting a widowed Episcopal rector, who, ignorant
of her predicament, states that he will never marry again because
he expects to be reunited with his wife after death. But Barbara,
fearful for Jock's well-being, soon summons him back. Somewhat
mystified by her capriciousness, he returns. All goes well until a
few days later, when Barbara is forced to wait out a thunderstorm
in the little Gothic church where she was married. Her natural
claustrophobia and the power of the elements combine to erase
the healthy stability of the preceding few days. Unable to fight off
the morbid thoughts which beset her, Barbara is evercome with
the memory of her wedding and Val's words: "Death cannot part
us, Barbara"(517). When Jock gets to her, she is prostrate from
nervous exhaustion.

After her recovery, Jock feels a natural mixture of sympathy and disgust. When Barbara becomes rational, her first request is that he place her wedding ring on her finger. He naturally refuses, the ring drops to the floor, and he leaves. A final scene shows Barbara finding the ring on the hearth, blowing the ashes from it, and replacing it herself. Her blowing the ashes away symbolically renews the morbid love of the past, and her replacing the ring confirms it. It is also clear that the love for the dead will continue, as indicated by the ring, a symbol of eternal love. There is, however, no reason to think that Jock will not return, as he had done earlier in the story; for, four years later, in the sequel *Barbara Dering* (1892), he does precisely that. For the moment, however, readers had to content themselves with a dilemma that had not been completely resolved; for, though Barbara had apparently chosen the dead over the quick, it is difficult to believe that she had permanently repressed her will to live a rational life.

In any case, the lack of a satisfactory resolution is not so glaring an omission as might be imagined; for modern readers are likely to overlook, as did their counterparts in 1888, the explanatory subtitle which labels the work "a study." The author's apparent intention was not to take a stand on either side of the dilemma but to show the inner conflicts of a character grappling with the two forces. It is really the revelation of how a sensitive person of the period reacts to pressure from both sides, and how she attempts to give priority to reason and objectivity and to discard the sentiment and the morbidity that give the novel its reason for being.

Barbara's dilemma suggests, however, interpretations on at least two larger scales; and one of these accounts, at least in part, for the lack of resolution in the novel. One interpretation concerns Barbara's relationship to Amélie, which is more intimate than that shared by any prior heroine. On the surface, Barbara is attempting to choose between two men; but, in reality, her choice is between a sentimental attachment to the past and the practical acceptance of the reality of the present. Amélie had given the world several stories shaded by the rosy hues of the past as she imagined it, but she had offered in "Virginia of Virginia" a story infused with present reality. She now had an important decision to make: whether to continue with the past and the sentimental emphasis which usually accompanied its depiction or to treat contemporary subjects realistically. Had this question been decided

in her own mind, then in all probability it could have been satisfactorily settled in the novel. As it was, it remained unsettled in
both her mind and her book.

On a still larger scale, the divided mind in *The Quick or the
Dead?* reflected the tastes of the American reading public which
by 1888 were gradually dividing between those who preferred
the sentimental oozings of the popular magazines (still the vast
majority) and a growing minority who preferred more Realism. It
had, after all, been but three years since the famous discussion
concerning an imaginary, but typical, popular romance of the mid-
1880's had taken place around the Boston dinner table of the
Brahmin Bromfield Corey in William Dean Howells' *The Rise of
Silas Lapham.* A Miss Kingsbury asks Corey's guests if they have
read *Tears, Idle Tears,* which she describes as "perfectly heart-
breaking" and as containing "such a dear old-fashioned hero and
heroine . . . who keep dying for each other all the way
through. . . ." [9] Her description is met by mixed reaction; and,
by the end of the discussion, hers is the single voice for the de-
fense. Opposing her have been Corey's daughter Nanny, who re-
names the book *Slop, Silly Slop,* and Sewell, the minister, who
heatedly tells Miss Kingsbury that "those novels with old-fashioned heroes and heroines in them are . . . ruinous!" "The novel-
ists might be the greatest possible help to us if they painted life as
it is," he adds, "and human feelings in their true proportion and
relation, but for the most part they have been and are altogether
noxious" (162).

One may regard this conversation as representing the division
among the well educated of the current reading public. The Sentimental is preferred by a middle-aged woman, whose knowledge
of love has been inhibited by her spinsterhood and by her pro-
tected Brahmin upbringing. Realism is defended by Sewell,
whose experience has embraced life on a variety of levels. More
significantly, however, it is preferred by Nanny Corey, a member
of the coming generation, who already shows some of the signs of
the liberated woman by refusing to look at life through the rose-
colored glasses of Sentimentality.

Such a division of public taste is virtually unresolvable. Preference for the Realistic as opposed to the Sentimental, or vice versa,
is no more unified today than it was in 1888, even though in the
intervening years the balance has become heavily weighted to-

ward Realism. On the personal levels of the intellect and the artistry of Amélie Rives, however, resolution was ultimately possible; but it did not come immediately. For ten years after the publication of *The Quick or the Dead?* her work showed a decided mixture of the Sentimental and the Realistic. Eventually she settled upon the Realistic vein, and consistent laudatory reviews indicated that her choice was wise.

It is tempting to speculate, however, what these ten years might have produced had the reaction to *The Quick or the Dead?* been different. It was her boldest step in Realism to date, and its praise was based largely upon this quality. What she failed to realize, however—and what her experience of writing sentimental stories for popular magazines had failed to teach her—was that the champions who brandished the sword of Realism in Victorian America were wielding a two-edged weapon. For every thrust which gained ground for the new Realistic order a wound was dealt to the popular conscience which evoked strident retaliation. The Realists—Howells, James, and Clemens—had forthrightly met the foe several times before 1888. In all probability they anticipated reprisal even before they published the works which provoked it. But not so with Amélie Rives: she was an unsuspecting innocent whose forthcoming slaughter could have been conceived neither in her wildest dreams nor in any of her far-fetched early stories.

III   *Sound and Fury: Spring, 1888*

The April, 1888, issue of *Lippincott's* had been in the hands of readers but a short while when a strange cry went up. It screamed the one word which the public dreaded most: "Immorality." *The Quick or the Dead?*, it charged, was built upon an immoral premise: widows of a few months did not debate whether or not to marry again. According to the canons of popular morality, there was nothing to debate about; the proper thing for a bereaved spouse to do was to don her mourning garb and dote upon past happiness. Like the Episcopal rector in the novel, one should look to reunion in the afterlife and not think about the anticipated fifty years remaining in this one. The second alleged example of immorality was Barbara's impassioned entreaty to Jock: "Kiss me!"(511).

The novel was preached about from pulpits; it was likewise praised and damned in magazines and newspapers. The New York *Times* called it "ridiculous trash" [10] and made slighting reference to its "essential vulgarity." Letters, poured in to the publisher in great profusion, were so filled with vitriol that Amélie was forced to ask that they be screened before being sent to her. Sympathetic critics joined in the fray. The poet Richard Hovey wrote her that he considered the public's reaction "an unmitigated outrage." [11] *Lippincott's* ran sympathetic follow-up reviews.

Still the storm raged, though not without some compensations. Sales of the book climbed, eventually reaching over three hundred thousand. Then the parodists conferred the left-handed compliment usually offered by their genre: increased popularity of the original work. The most famous travesty was the anonymous *Be Quick and Be Dead*, [12] claiming to be by "Ophélia Hives, (with the accent on)." Its two-hundred-pound protagonist who, "in a grassy sense . . . was a widow," (7) has to decide whether to remarry her rich husband (who refuses to "be quick and be dead") or his penniless leech of a cousin. Another was by Thomas Cooper De-Leon, a professed Rives admirer, who entitled his *The Rock or the Rye: An Understudy*. [13] It concerns the dilemma of Agamemna Comefret, who must decide whether to stay married to Rock, who is losing badly at the New Orleans racetrack, or to marry Rye, "his identical twin cousin." Both parodies were witty, and both focused on the unusual style of the original. For instance, DeLeon describes Agamemna as follows: "The Tyrian dyes in the kaleidoscopic imagery upon the dorsality of the dolphin *in articulo mortis,* was never so brilliant varihuey as the tints that chased each other over the girlly cheeks of the misdirected wife! In their encrimsoning reflections, glowing sunsetly, even her massed curls seemed a shade less wildly rubrant than before" (11).

In retrospect, one recognizes the cries of the moralists, the prudes, and the parodists as overreactions. The ultimate intensity of the furor was largely the result of a chain reaction. As time went on, critical voices found fuel for their fires not from any honest opinions based upon an individual understanding of the novel but from one another. That they came to lose a true sense of perspective and were caught by the force of the furor is well illustrated by an anecdote which the author herself related afterward. A number of years after the controversy had quieted, she was being entertained at the home of Price Collier. When her famous novel was mentioned, he proffered that he had written one of the few decent reviews. Though Amélie expressed her doubt, he hurried to his study to get a copy only to return with a sheepish look and the admission that there were parts which he would not like her to see.[14]

It was the age-old case of a mild breeze being whipped into tempest force; and, as is the case with most man-made tempests, one is afterward left puzzled as to why it should have occurred. An article appearing in *The Bookman* in 1912, a full twenty-four years after the shouting had died, cited the work for having founded the "semi-erotic genre" in the American novel; but the writer also admitted that the novel "would probably not cause the slightest ripple of excitement" had it been written at the later time.[15]

Time is surely the key to the scandalous success of *The Quick or the Dead?*, but it also accounts for its significance in American literature, as was brought out in the review of Edgar Fawcett which appeared in *Lippincott's* several months after the novel. Fawcett's was a voice of sane understanding in the midst of frenzied furor, and his review is the most completely developed and most evenly balanced of the many that appeared.[16] Though he basically liked the novel and recognized the innocence of the author's motives, he likewise sensed why her latest work had evoked the public's wrath. She had written the story, he said, "without stopping to consider what dangers, with a writer of her strongly romantic trend, must surround any such literary exploit unless a good deal of discriminative caution be made to accompany it. . . ."

To exercise this caution required that one be sensitive to the sometimes subtle differences between what the age would and would not tolerate in the way of Realistic detail. Fawcett realized these distinctions as Amélie could never have done from the safe isolation of Castle Hill. He saw that the current age did not require that emotion be cloaked in euphemism, as had the one fifty years before; but he was aware of a somewhat hypocritical sense of propriety which allowed for only "near Realism," or Realism without frankness. Warner Berthoff, a modern critic, has summarized some of the more prominent breaches of this code in the decade before *The Quick or the Dead?* appeared:

It is difficult to imagine the hostility aroused in the high-minded by only a small degree of common candor in books. Wrapping up unpleasant facts in a thoroughly "moral plot" did not remove objections. Howells got into trouble for dealing with adultery and divorce in *A Modern Instance* (1882), Mark Twain for using bad grammar and natural morals in *Huckleberry Finn* (1884), Jacob Riis for documenting with actual cases his statement of how the "other half" really lives. Even "Daisy Miller" was refused by the American editor to whom it was first offered. "Let only the truth be told, *and not all the truth*" [italics mine]—so said Joseph Kirkland, a self-styled devotee of the new realism. . . .[17]

The years following the publication of *The Quick or the Dead?* were to yield works of fiction that told more and more of the bare truth that Kirkland had warned against. Stephen Crane's epochal *Maggie: A Girl of the Streets* appeared in 1893; Frank Norris's *McTeague* in 1899; and Theodore Dreiser's *Sister Carrie* in 1900. These stories of slum life, prostitution, man's bestiality, and a Godless universe went a long way toward penetrating the curtain of propriety which had veiled such themes before. Reading Naturalists like Crane, Dreiser, and Norris makes the work of Clemens, Howells, and James appear quite innocuous—and *The Quick or the Dead?* innocence itself.

Though the public reaction to the novel was an ironic stroke of fate, it left Amélie flabbergasted. For a time, she was forced to recoil to the safety of the Sentimental mode. Also, the furor very likely prompted her to move her wedding date forward from October;[18] for she and Chanler were married on June 15 at Castle Hill in the presence of a few close family members and friends. A long wedding trip was postponed, probably for reasons concerning the bride's career. In midsummer the galley proofs of *Herod and Mariamne*, her first published drama, were ready; and the work appeared in *Lippincott's* in the September issue. There were also plans to publish *The Quick or the Dead?* in book form.[19] In November, the novel was dramatized (with little success)[20] on Broadway. In January came Amélie's first adventure into social issues, when she offered a hundred-dollar prize for the best essay on child labor written during the year. Because of all this activity, a proper wedding journey had to wait until spring.

IV   Herod and Mariamne (*1888*)

At the end of Fawcett's review of *The Quick or the Dead?*, he mentioned having seen the galley proofs of the drama *Herod and Mariamne*. After calling it "a tragedy of uneven yet often astonishing vigor," he criticized Herod as being "too unrelievedly ferocious and lurid." "Miss Rives can always draw women more firmly and satisfactorily than she can draw men," he added, "an evidence, I think, that she 'looks into her heart and writes.' " [21] A reading of Amélie Rives's work through *The Quick or the Dead?* easily bears out Fawcett's final statement. Female characters, obvious projections of the author herself, eclipse males. This characteristic is understandable with an author whose sheltered upbringing had afforded contact with few members of the opposite sex. Her closest companions were her sisters, Gertrude and Landon; governesses; and her cousin Louisa Pleasants, whom she called her closest friend.

Such, however, is not the case with *Herod and Mariamne*. There are moments when the male protagonist may resemble the overpowering Herod of the fourteenth-century "mystery plays," but there is no doubt that he is the dominant character of the drama. He is, moreover, the author's first significant male creation. Her Herod seems, therefore, to represent a significant step forward in character creation. Yet, one is cautious about describing either him or the play as a whole in superlatives because of the obvious derivation of both from Shakespeare's *Othello*. Like Othello, Herod loves "not wisely, but too well." He is more impetuous than the Moor and more suspicious, but his adamant adherence to an opinion is almost an exact parallel. To develop the comparison, one finds another Desdemona in Mariamne, whose love for her husband is pure and whose meek subordination to him is frequently seen during the first three acts. There are a number of Iagos: Alexandra, Mariamne's mother, who hates Herod; Cypros, Herod's mother; and Salome, his sister, both of whom hate Mariamne. The motive of this in-law hatred is jealousy, jealousy arising from the fact Herod has deposed high-priest Hyrcanus II and has been exalted to the kingship by Mark Antony.

Such are the facts found in Josephus, the chief source for the play; but they are made plausible in the drama by Herod's jealous love for Mariamne and by his impetuous nature, which derives from an insecurity of mind and position. Given this basic nature and the family infighting already described, Herod is in a position of hopeless vulnerability throughout the play. Early in the play, he asks Mariamne, "Would to heaven I knew what loving means to thee!" She answers:

> It means to put myself beyond myself,
> To think of him I love in that self's stead,
> To be sleep's enemy because of him,
> Because of him to be a friend of pain,
> To have no thought, no wish, no dream, no memory,
> That is not servant to him; to forget
> All earlier loves in his,—all hates, all wrongs;
> Being meek to him, though proud unto all others;
> Gentle to him, though to all others harsh;
> To him submissive, though unto high heaven
> Something rebellious. Last, to keep my patience
> And bear his doubts, who have his children borne.[22]

Mariamne's submissive loyalty to Herod is uppermost in her mind. But even such a seemingly ideal love cannot give him sustained happiness. On the contrary, he gives orders for Mariamne's execution twice in the first three acts. The first time, his mother, Cypros, has led him to believe that Mariamne and Mark Antony are conspiring to kill him. The second time, Salome, his sister, accuses Mariamne of having an affair with her husband, Joseph. In both instances, Herod soon finds Mariamne innocent and begs forgiveness; but she emerges the second time from her role as a passive wife to warn him that "Once to doubt is ever to be doubtful"(341).

These words are prophetic. He has his innocent brother-in-law Joseph executed in retaliation for Salome's scheming. Then she, realizing that he is in a state of insane passion, tells him that Mariamne is trying to poison him. He immediately orders Mariamne's execution, and Salome is for the moment triumphant. But Mariamne is able to break her bonds and stab Salome before being led to the block. As she walks to her death, she tells the tearful servant Sohemus, "No tears, good Sohemus, / Mine eyes are dry as are these breasts of mine, / Which once did nourish princes. Cease, I pray thee. / I'll walk alone, a queen unto the last" (385).

Herod's mind is now completely unstrung. He gives repeated commands to have Mariamne brought to him, so he may "shake the stars from out their blackened sockets / To light our bridal bed. . . ." Only at the very end of the play can his demented mind grasp the enormity of the havoc caused by his own weakness of character and by the circumstances which have exacerbated it. And it is at this point that Fawcett's assessment of Herod as "too unrelievedly ferocious and lurid" seems justified. Act V is considerably longer than need be, and Herod's final insane rantings tend to obscure the more temperate character of the first three acts. He is, of course, impetuous throughout, and he often comes to regret his hasty judgments; but he can also be tender. For instance, in Act II, when he finds that Mariamne is innocent of a suspected liaison with Mark Antony, he returns to her a chastened penitent. She replies, "Now thou'rt king indeed,— / Now Herod at his best"(333). The same scene shows him a gallant lover, as when he addresses Mariamne: "God's heart, girl, thou art twenty times more sweet / Than all thy dear Samaria's sunkissed fruits. / Thy lips! Once more thy lips! . . ." (330).

These facets are obviously those of a character much more human than that found in the medieval "mystery plays." In them, Herod was shown as the Satanic slayer of the innocents. It is just possible that Amélie Rives knew of these plays and that they exerted some influence on her depiction of Herod in the closing scenes. It is certain, however, that her chief influence was Elizabethan tragedy, which in general featured a more rounded, refined protagonist than did the medieval plays, which usually contained mere caricatures. Moreover, the central theme of *Herod and Mariamne* is the tragic love of two people whose natures make fulfillment and communication impossible. In the final analysis, it is a dual tragedy; both principals experience an inevitable fall, and both are exalted characters who are sympathetic to the audience.

The language of the play is, appropriately, an adaptation of Elizabethan blank verse. For the most part, it is dignified and controlled, if at times repetitious. Any playwright would be proud to have written lines such as Sohemus's statement, "When queens quarrel kings are kings in vain"(306); or Cypros's observation, "A Herod laughs where many a man would weep"(313); or Hyrcanus's warning that "Who rouses hate must look for hell to follow" (317). The magnificence of Mariamne's speech in which she describes first seeing Herod rivals Enobarbus's famous description of Antony's first view of Cleopatra (*Antony and Cleopatra*, II, ii, 190–245). Mariamne has first seen Herod at a festival:

> At last,
> When almost we were tired of watching youths
> Draw bows or brandish spears, he came. His horse,
> A coal-black Arab, trapped in beaten gold,
> As though dark Night had borrowed of bright Day,
> Chafed at the reins and reared. At that the king,
> Herod, thy father, dashed his mighty fist
> Against the brute's strained chest, then, loosing rein,
> Poised lithely, with his javelin aloft,
> Keen on the changing air onward they swooped,
> Straight on, with singing hair and hoofs a-thunder,
> Like to a wind made visible. (329)

It may be argued that more credit is due the creators of a mode of speech than to those who adapt it. Surely much of the beauty of these lines and phrases derives from the Elizabethan style which they emulate. An equally impressive argument, however, could be waged over placing adaptations in a genre by themselves. There is, after all, wide variation in quality among adaptations, which shows that not all artists are capable of doing them well. Seen as an adaptation, *Herod and Mariamne* is an especially high accomplishment. Its author took a foreign character which none of the major Elizabethan dramatists had treated, and she adapted him and formed him to the mold of Elizabethan drama, from which she was separated by three centuries.

Though the shadow of Shakespeare's *Othello* looms rather more vividly then one might wish, the treatment of the tragic love story is Amélie Rives's alone, as is the dialogue. It is one thing to use an Elizabethan patois when narrating the adventures of stock Elizabethans, as had been done in "A Brother to Dragons"; but it is something else to create the dialogue of complex characters involved in convoluted emotional crises. Seen in this light, the adapted Elizabethan style is one of the strongest points in the play. On the whole, *Herod and Mariamne* was a fitting end to a year of busy literary activity. It was also a harbinger of the next year's triumphs.

CHAPTER 3

An Innocent Abroad

A MÉLIE and Archie Chanler sailed for Europe on April 13, 1889. Though it was the bride's first trip abroad, she lost no time in making friends. After stopping briefly in Paris, where she was enthusiastically received by Chanler's cousin, Madame de Stuers, they set out for England, where she received what was to prove a far more meaningful reception. During the 1887 season at Newport she had met Lady Desborough, in whose country house, Taplow Court, she and Chanler were guests. Lord and Lady Desborough were members of a large group whose activities were much publicized in the press.

I *"The Souls": Summer, 1889*

This collection of friends and political associates, while not formally organized, were often together, and they were most selective about whom they admitted from the outside. Many of the friendships dated back several years to the undergraduate days of certain male members. Several diverse political opinions were represented. There were progressive conservatives like Randolph Churchill and Arthur Balfour, as well as outspoken liberals like Herbert Asquith, who later married Margot Tennant, one of the most flamboyant young women in the group. About the time of the Chanlers' arrival, the coterie was labeled "The Souls" by one of its members.[1] Though probably conceived in jest, this appellation soon became fixed in both the minds of the members and of outsiders.

The "Souls'" exercise of intellectual snobbery and their preference for the avant-garde gave credence to this title. They considered games like baccarat and bridge to be lowbrow, and they indulged, for instance, in something they called "styles," the object of which was to write passages in the style of a given author.[2]

Avowed friends of Estheticism, they thought Oscar Wilde devil-
ishly clever; but they were also adamant in excluding him from
their number. They wanted, in short, the safety of an elite social
position as well as the freedom to transcend that position in the
exercise of artistic taste.

The unofficial leader of the group was George Curzon, whose
life style was typical of the members as a whole. He had recently
gained popularity as a witty young member of Parliament, and he
ultimately became governor-general of India and chancellor of
Oxford University. At the same time, in the words of his official
biographer, "[he] admired beauty in women with all the ardor of
his artistic temperament, and he courted their admiration in return. . . ." [3] He was usually successful in obtaining the favor he
courted, as is evidenced by his friendship with Elinor Glyn after
the death of his wife.

Both of these women were beautiful, and both were literary. In
the new Mrs. Chanler, he found the same combination; and he
and the other "Souls" accepted her and Archie as part of their
circle, a distinction given to only two other Amercans. [4] In a doggerel after-dinner speech of July 10, 1889, in which Curzon celebrated each individual present, he referred to Amélie as "Virginia's marvellous daughter / Having conquered the States / She's
been blown by the Fates / To conquer us over the water." [5]

In addition to her many new friends among the "Souls," Amélie
soon made a number of acquaintances among the English literati.
Foremost among these was Oscar Wilde, [6] who inscribed a copy
of *The Happy Prince* to her as "her sincere admirer." She also
came to know Thomas Hardy, who complimented her on "Virginia of Virginia"; Henry James, who pled with her to come to live
in England; and George Meredith, who thought she bore a physical resemblance to Algernon Swinburne as a young man. [7]

II   The Witness of the Sun: *1889*

It is unfortunate that these authors' opinions of *The Witness of
the Sun* have not survived. Published just before Amélie left America, it was the first of her many novels set in Europe. And, considering that she had never been there, her feeling for the Italian
Riviera setting is extremely fine. Very likely, though, these writers
would have been more interested in the theme of this book, which

was more bizarre than anything she had yet written or would write. It represented a foray into a distant corner of the realm of Realism, which would have been considered prurience itself had the critics understood its full implications.

On the surface, *The Witness of the Sun* is the story of the young Russian novelist Vladimir Nadrovine and of his attempt to cut the unusually strong cord which binds him to his possessive mother so that he may enjoy a normal love relationship with Ilva Demarini, the Rives heroine. But one does not have to go far below this surface to see the mother's insane jealousy as a symptom of incest. Just after Vladimir has sealed his engagement to Ilva by the gift of his family ring, Madame Nadrovine appears. No sooner has she passionately kissed her son on the mouth than she begins reminiscing about the marks which his toothless gums left on her breasts when he was an infant, and she vows to murder any woman who threatens to take him away from her. Even at the end of the novel, when she is delirious from the fever that is about to end her life, she babbles about the happy days when the infant Vladimir fed at her breasts.

Amélie almost certainly failed to realize the full psychological ramifications of Madame Nadrovine's love for her son, and this assumption is confirmed by the fact that none of the book's reviewers realized it either. By 1889 Freudian psychology was neither a fully developed set of theories nor a recognized implement for the analysis of literature. Literary characters said and did things quite oblivious of what their words and deeds might betray about the unconscious psyches of either themselves or their authors. Had the critics of *The Quick or the Dead?* been aware of such a critical approach, they would surely have set up a hue and cry even louder than that they had raised over the earlier book, and this time for more justifiable reason. As it was, *The Witness of the Sun* was reviewed sparsely, and the consensus of these occasional criticisms was simply that the novel was a decidedly minor performance.

Perhaps the stance of the critics was to some degree influenced by the scandalous success of *The Quick or the Dead?* the preceding year. It would have been easy for any book written at this time to be swept aside by the wake of the earlier work, especially when the new one did not surpass it in sensational value. On the other hand, *The Witness of the Sun* contained a number of re-

deeming features, ones overlooked in the attitude of anticlimax
which seemed to dominate the judgment of its critics. First, this
book, more than any before it, emphasized character over plot.
With few exceptions, incidents occur by the assertion of dominant
personality traits among the characters. Plot, therefore, is not a
matter of clever manipulation of incidents by the author, but a
natural cause-effect evolution: Vladimir's courtship continues un-
abated after his mother enters the story, and all goes well until he
discovers that his mother has a lover (Ilva's father). Partly out of
shock and partly out of jealousy, he duels with Signor Demarini,
who falls and kills himself. Now, thinking that he has lost his
mother's love as well as Ilva's, he flees, even though Ilva is willing
to forgive his part in her father's death; but his mother discovers
him just as he is about to take vows as a Trappist monk.

Only at this point does the author seem to falter in her narrative. Evidently unable to leave her hero in his cloister with the
crisis in his love unresolved, and not seeing how events can be
terminated naturally, she resorts to some rather jejune plot manipulations which mar the last twenty or so pages of the book.
Just after the ordination ceremony, during which Madame Nadrovine has stood outside the chapel and cursed the initiating order,
she goes down the hill and wanders into a little tavern. Finding
the owner ill with delirium tremens and a raging fever, she, in an
unprecedented and unbelievable act of charity, nurses him back
to health and falls fatally ill with his fever in the process. Then, as
if by a *deus ex machina,* Ilva appears with her little cousin. The
child immediately walks onto some quicksand, Vladimir rushes to
her, flings her to safety, and becomes trapped himself. Ilva, realizing his plight, rushes into the mire, joins him in a passionate em-
brace, and thence in death. The pages containing this contrived
Liebestod are just what Ernest Hemingway said the final third of
Huckleberry Finn was: "cheating." Yet, these constitute barely
one-tenth of a novel which in numerous other ways is a credit-
able performance.

The Witness of the Sun contains the author's most controlled use
of symbolism thus far. The key symbol, used throughout as a uni-
fying device, is the sun itself. Introduced in the inscription on the
ring which Vladimir gives Ilva—*Esto sol testis* ("Let the sun be a
witness")—it means, he tells her, that a man should "strive to keep
his life so clean and without reproach that the sun can search

every cranny without bringing unwholesome or ugly facts to light. . . ." [8] In a later scene, Vladimir's mother has to shade her eyes from the early rays of the sun just after he tells her that Demarini died as the sun was rising (175). In all three of these instances the sun symbolizes truth—that which Vladimir seeks in his novels and in his love, that which his mother cannot face, and that which subdues Demarini. As Madame Nadrovine follows Vladimir to the chapel, the sun is shown in eclipse, a ball of "sodden crimson behind a bank of dense gray . . ."(214). By the time they reach the ceremony, the sun has disappeared (215), indicating that the awful truth of Demarini's death, which the rising sun had revealed to him earlier, is to be obscured by the newly found truth of religion, but that this truth is contained in the cold, damp cloister. In the final scene, the sun has a "level light"(246), suggesting the equilibrium of the moment in which all is set right. This interpretation is borne out by the final sentence: "The Sun had been a witness"(248).

Though unnaturally evolved, the final union of the lovers is a thoroughly believable action. It brings into sharper focus than any earlier work had done the theme of the endurance of love after death. In the final scene of "Virginia of Virginia," Virginia Herrick dies expressing her love for Roden. Barbara Pomfret in *The Quick or the Dead?* accepts the Episcopal minister's belief that one can be reunited in the afterlife with a spouse, a fact which strongly, though morbidly, delays her acceptance of Jock. For Ilva and Vladimir, however, the choice is freely made; and the "level light" of the sun symbolizes approval of the universe. Although their earthly happiness lasts only minutes, it suggests the Browning-like belief that worthwhile undertakings started on the earth may be continued in the afterlife. The theme appears again and again in Amélie's later stories and dramas. And forty-seven years after the quicksand had enveloped the fictional Ilva and Vladimir, the aged Amélie, while waiting for her own death just after the passing of her second husband, requested that a family friend have carved on her gravestone the line from the Song of Solomon (VIII:6) "Love is strong as death." [9]

Just now, however, the strength of love was about to be tested in her personal life; and the indications were that it would prove considerably less strong than death. One of the purposes which she and Chanler had in mind for their belated wedding trip was an extended stay in Paris, where she was to study art. Before this sojourn, they were to travel in the late summer through Europe; and during this tour the first known friction of their marriage began to develop. Among the Chanler papers in the Duke University Library is a fragment of dialogue written in Amélie's hand that is too short to show much development, yet it concerns an argument between the two over an accusation Archie has made that Amélie had been untruthful to him about something. At the end of the fragment (which was written in Kissingen, Germany, and dated August 26, 1889), Archie reminds her that, by her own admission, she had been untruthful to him in Newport.

Just what prompted his accusation is not known; but, from subsequent indications, trouble was imminent. Sometime in the autumn Amélie's closest friend Louisa Pleasants joined the Chanlers, and probably about this time she and Amélie went to Paris alone. It was gradually becoming obvious that the Chanlers shared more interests apart than together. By the middle of December Chanler had joined Miss Pleasants and Amélie in quarters on the Place de la Madeleine, but he was soon planning a safari to Africa which he did not wish her to know about. Another separation came early in 1890 when he left for the United States to establish the Paris Prize Fund, which offered a deserving American artist a stipend of nine hundred dollars for a year's study in the French capital.

Amélie remained on the Place de la Madeleine to study, but little is known of this year, except that she studied under Charles Lasar, a pupil of Gerôme and one of the best-known painting masters of the day. By March, she had gone on a holiday to Algiers, where she caused a slight ripple of excitement in the press when Jules Renaud, a young art student, committed suicide because of unrequited love for her. By winter, she was back in Paris; and Chanler had returned. But, frequently ill during this period, she was in San Remo for her health by January, 1891. From San Remo, Louisa Pleasants wrote Chanler on January 29, chiding him for not having written Amélie and quoting her as having said "I understand him *perfectly*[.] I know just how he feels—but oh! I do *wish* he would write—It seems so long. . . ." [10] Amiable although this separation might have been, this letter indicates a lack of communication which was never improved.

By the time the Chanlers returned to the United States on August 24, 1891, news of a marital rift had leaked to the papers; for a

squib in the November Baltimore *Times* wryly stated that
"Amelia [*sic*] Rives says her husband proposed to her five times
before she accepted. With what sincere yearning must that poor
man now wish he'd had lockjaw just after the fourth applica-
tion." [11] Nevertheless, she and Chanler returned to Castle Hill; and
she stated to the press that she would study painting for another
six months (Lasar was to join them) and that she would not attempt another novel until her course of study was over.

III   According to St. John (*1891*)

Amélie's decision to give full time to painting was probably
wise, at least for the moment. She was a talented artist whose
work earned high compliments from contemporary critics. However, reviews of *According to St. John,* the first installment of
which had appeared in the August, 1891, *Cosmopolitan,*[12] were
anything but complimentary. Their denunciation seems as justified as was the praise of the art critics.

Obviously reflecting the author's experiences in Paris, *According to St. John* is the story of Jean Carter—like Amélie, an American innocent abroad among the evils of Paris. Jean studies the
violin and lives in the same *pension* with an artist named Farrance, his wife, and their infant son. Mrs. Farrance is very ill with
consumption, and just before her death she tells Jean that she
would like for her and her husband to marry.

She dies a few weeks later; and, after the wake and the funeral
(which are described with a profusion of maudlin detail), Farrance leaves. When he returns several months later, he goes
through his wife's effects and finds a letter from her expressing the
wish that he marry Jean. By this time he and Jean have had several serious conversations which indicate that they clearly have
different ideas. He believes in a mechanical God who does not
offer his subjects eternal life; Jean, like her ancestral Rives heroines, believes in a benevolent deity who allows love to continue
after death. Farrance finally persuades Jean to marry him by saying that, while he can never love her as he had loved his wife
(man is unable to love in a particular way but once but has the
capacity to love in many different ways), he has a special way of
loving her.

Probably unintentionally, Farrance is the best-drawn character in the book. Mrs. Farrance is a sympathetic enough character in the few scenes in which she appears, but these glimpses are too fragmentary and brief for a well-rounded character to emerge. Jean Carter, the most lackluster of the Rives heroines, probably reflects her creator's tortured uncertainties of this period; for Jean gropes her way through the action of the novel, unable to determine the firm course that most of her antitypes had devised. However, Farrance, because of his essential nature, is appropriately understated. Without ever literally saying so, the author gives the distinct impression that he is not a particularly talented artist and that he lacks spiritual depth. It follows, moreover, that he lacks sensitivity, a failing demonstrated in both his marriages.

Though realizing that his love for Jean is different from that for his first wife, he keeps comparing the two. In the first few weeks he becomes quite frustrated by the disparity, so he confides to his diary that his life is one long hypocrisy. Jean finds the diary just after learning that a painting for which she has posed (for a few desperately needed francs) has attracted more favorable attention than one painted by Farrance, which both of them had hoped would be a financial success. Her sense of guilt and her disappointment for Farrance convince her that suicide is the only answer to her unhappy plight. However, her final rationale for taking the fatal dose of morphine comes, of all places, from the Scriptures (John XV:13): "Greater love hath no man than this, that a man lay down his life for his friends."

It is difficult to consider the novel without considering the suicide at the end; for Amélie never committed in her entire career so egregious a literary offense. One is really supposed to believe, apparently, that a wife should commit suicide just because her husband thinks his marriage is hypocritical. Judged in terms of "Virginia of Virginia" or *Herod and Mariamne*, this book is certainly a regression. One possible redeeming feature, pointed out by one reviewer,[13] is the picture that the author delineates of student life in Paris. Even conceding this attribute, the story is the worst Amélie ever wrote.

Some of the cleverest and most cutting reviews were leveled at this novel. For example, the ever lively *Spirit of the Times* called Jean Carter "no credit to her sex, her state and her country. It is sad to see such talents as Mrs. Chanler possesses wasted upon a book which, when she is twenty years older, she would not allow her daughter to read. . . ." [14] The most penetrating review appeared in *The Nation*. By pointing the accusing finger at the author's lack of moral vision, it readily explains such weak features as character motivation. "The author's notions about morals have never appeared to be conspicuously sound," said the reviewer, "but since in this story she makes a distinct effort to be virtuous, almost chaste, we observe with regret her confusion about morals, in the widest meaning, in the perception of right and wrong. . . ." He cited as examples the fact that Mrs. Farrance has never loved her husband and that she has harbored love for another man while married to him. Also, the moralistic Jean "understands" why Farrance cannot love her even though he is married to her. This causes the reviewer to "mourn that she chose to play the fiddle instead of composing treatises of pure reason." [15]

IV *The Artist in Transition: 1892*

One is tempted to speculate about the reasons *According to St. John* should have been the failure it was at the time that it was. Within the realm of possibility is the fact that Amélie was experiencing a traumatic initiation from a vicarious view of love as seen in *The Quick or the Dead?* into an only too-real knowledge of unhappy marriage and that this process had left her uncertain about the moral obligation which a wife should have for her husband. Or, as she was ill much of the time during the writing of the story, she may simply have not thoroughly thought through the problem.

Whatever the reason, or reasons, the year following her return to America (November, 1892) was the most important year in her artistic life—not for what it produced in published titles but for what it produced in the author's mind and temperament. In the early months of the winter, her painting progressed rapidly under Lasar's tutelage; but she became ill within a few weeks with one of her now frequent rheumatic attacks and had to interrupt her work with a stay at Hot Springs, a popular Virginia spa.

Much of this time Chanler was in New York, presumably tending to his law practice.[16] His wife's condition was reported by letters—often written by Louisa Pleasants, as Amélie was too weak to write.[17] Though scant evidence, these letters lead one to assume that the earlier marriage difficulties persisted. It is difficult to believe that the husband of a happy marriage could remain separated from his wife at such a time just to look after a law practice which was never a necessary part of his livelihood. Of course, he had been absent from her during much of her European sojourn, and part of this time she had also been ill. In the next two years he continued the same pattern, despite her frequently expressed desire to see him. Just now, being unwell and receiving harsh criticism for *According to St. John,* she most probably felt a stronger need for him than ever. Moreover, she was grappling with the dilemma of whether to pursue a career in painting or to continue writing.

By the autumn of 1892, it was obvious that she had made the important decision of continuing her literary career. Her resolve was marked by the publication of *Barbara Dering,* a sequel to *The Quick or the Dead?* It clearly outshone the earlier novel, as well as all the preceding fiction, not only in its vivid Realism, but in its well-controlled plot, in its language (now largely freed from past emotionalism), and in its objective portrayal of the marriage theme. Barbara Pomfret has come a long way from the morbid widow of *The Quick or the Dead?:* she is now more objective and poised and her reason has subdued her emotion.

Barbara Dering indicates, then, that Amélie had once again displayed the strength of character which so often characterized her artistic development and her personal life. She had turned a period of illness and questioning into firm resolution. She had emerged a mature artist. More importantly, she had arrived at this eminence largely without anyone's help, least of all Chanler's.

The year preceding *Barbara Dering* had dramatized the vast differences in their natures. Being a woman of strong pride and talent, she needed a companion who would help her find fulfillment in these areas. Instead, she was yoked to a partner long accustomed to having his own desires and whims indulged (a good example is the African safari). Worse still, he was either incapable of, or uninterested in, indulging others. This is not to say that he did not exhibit such redeeming qualities as generosity and charity toward the less fortunate; it is merely to explain why neither he nor Amélie could expect much lasting happiness while married to each other. Despite their difficulties, however, the marriage lasted another two years.

V Barbara Dering: *1892*

If an uninitiated reader were to seek out a single work of Amélie Rives which would most typically represent her entire output,
he would do well to select *Barbara Dering*, the novel which broke
the year's silence following her return from Europe. With the glaring exception of *According to St. John*, her artistic career showed
a growing maturity after the publication of the early naïve short
stories. As she progressed in the areas of style, characterization,
plotting, and various other technical aspects of fiction writing, her
work became increasingly Realistic and less sentimental. One may
safely hypothesize, therefore, that the strengths in one of Amélie
Rives's novels is proportionate to its Realistic qualities. *Barbara
Dering* contains more vivid Realism than any work of this experimental or developmental period, which ends in 1898; it also looks
ahead to the post-1900 period which produced primarily Realistic
works.

True enough, *Barbara Dering* contains an aftertaste of the old
sentimentality which had characterized and to some degree
marred earlier works, but it is presented in a context of satire. Its
author as well as her analogous protagonist are women no longer
dominated by situations; both exercise a poised self-control. In
comparison with Amélie's former heroines, Barbara as she appears
in this book is far superior. This heroine, like the author herself, represented the "new woman" at the turn of the century: robust, yet
sensitive, she was prepared to drink, as the Victorians' Omar
Khayyam had suggested, the wine of life down to the dregs. Her
robustness represented an exceedingly strong life force which sustained the body as well as the spirit. This woman liked the out-of-
doors; she rode and swam with great vigor, as Virginia Herrick
had done. These characteristics are easily portrayed, but not so
the emotional side; for, in portraying it, one could easily have
lapsed into sentimentality.

By the time Amélie created Barbara Dering, it is obvious that
she had learned a great deal about characterization. Barbara as
she appeared in *The Quick or the Dead?* was not a different personality, but in the earlier book she tended to be immature in
facing her dilemma. When she becomes Barbara Dering, however, she uses her intelligence and, as a result, appears a much

more solid character. Both she and Jock are kinetic characters who undergo tremendous growth in the course of the story. Characteristic of their old misunderstandings, they disagree about a sonnet of Dante Gabriel Rossetti which Barbara reads him one day soon after their marriage (which takes place early in the novel). The sonnet, "Her Love," ends with the lines, "Ah! who shall say she deems not loveliest / The hour of sisterly sweet hand-in-hand?" Jock impetuously tells her that he thinks these lines silly, for overt love-making is to be preferred to the subtle gesture. Though Barbara is hurt by his assertions, each finally apologizes to the other. Still, to Barbara, love must have sentiment and concern itself with the tenderness and the small detail of which Jock is disdainful.

In the midst of Barbara's sporadic unhappiness (the results of events like these), Eunice Bransby is introduced. She and her husband Godfrey serve a twofold purpose in the story: they are used (Godfrey in particular) for social satire and as foils to Barbara and Jock, for a wide emotional gap separates the four. In the beginning of the story, Barbara and Jock are the worldly sophisticates, the exact antitheses of the Bransbys, who are anachronistic Puritans in the most odious sense of the word. Though Godfrey is thoroughgoing in this trait, Eunice is dissatisfied; but she is so conditioned by his attitudes that she knows no way of overcoming them. The brilliant result, managed as well as any plot of Jane Austen, is that polarities develop between the Bransbys as those between the Derings disappear. Moreover, as the gap develops between the Bransbys, Eunice moves closer to the Derings; and the final result is that Godfrey Bransby is left by himself.

Just after Eunice is introduced into the story and gives Barbara comfort in her unhappiness, Jock (perhaps reminiscent of Chanler) leaves on a hunting trip with no advance notice to Barbara. He returns to find that Barbara has planned a dinner party for them and the Bransbys. This event brings the four together for the first time, and all differences are lucidly shown. During the next few months, the love of Barbara and Jock has its harmonious and discordant moments. Soon Barbara finds she is pregnant (though, for all the book's daring, this fact is merely hinted at—much like the seduction of Hardy's Tess of the D'Urbervilles).[18] Jock is much disturbed when the baby arrives, for he is jealous and possessive. He gradually softens, and loves the little girl,

Fairfax, just as jealously. Also, his love for Barbara becomes more firmly cemented than ever before, even though this closeness has been dearly bought by costly compromises in the two divergent personalities. The baby falls ill with a diphtheric throat infection; and, soon afterward, Jock catches a horrible cold, of the variety to which he is commonly susceptible. Barbara naturally has to attend to her child before Jock, and this makes his jealousy return.

Long interested in philanthropy, he decides to put Barbara's love to a test by asking her to leave the baby to accompany him on a trip to the West, where he is to study social problems. Like any good mother, she refuses, but he goes anyway, bidding her a cold farewell. When he is gone for months and seldom writes, she is naturally despondent; and, after one of his frigid letters, she returns to Val's grave and falls weeping upon it. A few days later she is out riding, and, as a storm is forming, her saddle girth breaks. Just then Godfrey Bransby comes by. He takes her into his trap; but, before they can reach his home, the horse becomes frightened at the lightning and rears, throwing him and cutting his leg badly. Barbara makes a tourniquet from her petticoat and saves his life. Then, as Jock is still away, she stays at the Bransbys' for several weeks.

During this time, much is made of the satiric role of Bransby. He is meant, obviously, to epitomize late-Victorian narrowness and self-righteousness and its inevitable hypocrisy. He disapproves of Barbara even to the color of her hair, which he finds too bright. But by this time Eunice, guided by Barbara, has begun to emerge from the shell he has tried to build around her and has become more assertive. Godfrey thinks her most unfeminine, for he believes that meekness and complete submission to the husband are the only course for a wife whose marriage has been made in his style of heaven. Barbara has made it clear that she is opposed to his fatuous notions—that a wife's natural emotions are to be developed properly, and not to be repressed. She tells him so while sitting beside him watching Lois and Winifred, his two little girls, playing below. Suddenly, he tries to kiss her, just as Eunice enters. Eunice greets his action with a quiet smile of satisfaction, knowing that at last she will have unquestioned leverage in her role as wife.

By this time, Barbara has become more convinced than ever of her love for Jock, and she also possesses a far deeper understanding of love. In the scene in which she had returned to Val's grave, she had come away with the realization that had "put aside all longing for supreme happiness in her present life. To be supremely strong for the happiness of others was now her heart's desire. . . ." [19] This resolve, plus Jock's profession of love and his promise that he has changed during the trip, makes one believe that their love will last and that the marriage will be happy. Also, Jock has found fulfillment in philanthropy; he wishes to help provide housing for factory girls (as Chanler was later to do).

The ending is quite brief. By the choice of a few facts, the author has been able to indicate what the eventual result will be; and, in this respect, she shows fine control and a mature understanding of a love relationship in which two people become less themselves and more of each other. It also indicates that she might well have found the solution to her own marital problems; but, as subsequent events show, she could never effectuate it.

In two former books, Amélie had capitalized on the plantation setting. While this atmosphere was most appealing to readers of the period, resembling, as it did, certain features of local-color writing, it was, nevertheless, out of keeping with the times. Castle Hill had been the exception rather than the rule during the Civil War, and the only value it offered as a setting to the average reader was as a vehicle for wistful nostalgia. Though the uncomplicated ease and the plenitude of antebellum life in the South are desirable in some ways, it is impossible to think of their ever returning; therefore, writing about such a way of life has limited value. However, *Barbara Dering* places plantation life in a new dimension. While still a part of this past existence, the characters step into the mainstream of late Victorian life. Barbara is involved with such issues as poverty, race, and the Feminist movement, which challenged both the South and the nation at large.

In 1892, one of the most basic of these questions was the modern woman: how she would fit into the social scheme of things and how she should relate not only to society in general but to her husband in particular. In *Barbara Dering*, one finds the author's ideas about this subject because husband and wife are portrayed more realistically than in any previous novel. Earlier Victorian women had been made both ideal and submissive. The etherealized wife portrayed in Coventry Patmore's *An Angel in the House* perhaps best represents the former state, while Eunice Bransby

represents, as well as any fictional wife of the era, the latter. She
has been subordinated to a prudish husband who for ten years has
advocated the notion that passion is animalistic. What latitude he
has noted in the Scriptures, he has narrowed to his own liking;
and it is no wonder that he fears Barbara:

> I have scarcely any doubt . . . that Mrs. Dering is the sort of
> woman who smokes cigarettes. I trust that you will be very
> guarded in your relations with her. She seems to me most un-
> feminine. That dagger-like arrangement that she wore in her hair
> struck me as disagreeably barbaric. Then she said several things
> that I considered decidedly irreverent, not to say verging on the
> blasphemous. That little anecdote . . . in which a child alludes
> to the Deity and Santa Claus in the same sentence, was, to me,
> intensely shocking. I also heard her say something about Rossetti.
> I hope, Eunice, that you will promise me that you will not let Mrs.
> Dering lead you into reading such authors. They are unwhole-
> some and unnatural. These overstrained sensations are not what
> men and women feel nowadays. I am devotedly thankful, my
> dear, that you are a sensible, practical, self-contained woman. You
> make me very happy indeed. (74–75)

To Barbara, and later to Eunice, this advice and these attitudes
are so much drivel. "We are not the bloodless creatures we are
generally thought to be," Barbara tells Eunice early in the story,

> Did you ever notice how, when a woman is considered very
> ardent, she is thought to be an exception to the general rule?
> Men are fond of saying we cannot keep a secret; and yet, when I
> think how well we have hidden that fact for ages, until even sci-
> entists speak of us as lacking in fire, I cannot help smiling at the
> popular belief! We are trained to be hypocrites. We are trained
> to regard all healthy, natural vivid impulses as unrefined, un-
> feminine, immodest. A girl likes even her lover to fancy that she
> yields unwillingly to his kisses. Oh, if I had a daughter, I would
> teach her that passion in love, in religion, in friendship, in patriot-
> ism, is a great, pure fire created by God, and not to be scorned
> by man. . . . (106)

The liberated woman has opinions on many subjects. In religion, for example, Barbara wishes to avoid theology and to love
people with sincere charity. In the midst of much *fin de siècle*

skepticism and an approaching crisis in the author's own life, there is in this story a true affirmation of faith. About her spokesman Barbara, Amélie has this to say: "In spite of all the pessimism and scepticism of the age, there was in her a wholesome fervor of belief in the final working together of all things for good, an unconquerable voice which spoke lowly in the silence of her soul, and which said, 'God is in me and I in Him . . .'" (242).

On the race question, Eunice states the opinion of many Southern intellectuals of the time: the Negro should not be subsidized but given the opportunity to improve his lot through his own endeavor. She even suggests that Godfrey build cabins for the Negroes who work for them, so that they as a family can have pride in a place of their own for which they should pay nominal rent in order to have a sense of accomplishment—an idea later expanded in *World's-End* and shown to be successful. This suggestion is not to be interpreted as meaning that Amélie stood for a leveling of the social classes, for she makes the opposite view very clear. Barbara, while saying in all sincerity that she would "be willing to give all I had to the poor, if I really thought that it would be anything but a penny dropped in mid-ocean," admits in the same breath, "I don't believe in equality any more than I would love a world that is one vast level. There must be valleys and mountains in human nature, as well as in landscapes. People are happier for looking up . . ." (191).

There is also much said and implied about late-Victorian men. Clearly, Jock is the ideal man as Amélie visualized him at the time. He is strong and completely virile; more importantly, he is a thorough realist and lacks sentimentality but not sentiment; for sentiment is the real theme of the novel. Both Barbara and Jock are self-centered in their feelings as the novel opens (a reflection back to the former story); but, as their marriage falters, both learn that sentiment must be removed from the self and be directed, ideally, toward the needs and feelings of others. At the end of the story, when Jock and Barbara's love becomes cemented firmly, Godfrey is still the same person he has been all through the story—the author's way of expressing her dislike of weakness and prudishness in males.

The ideal marriage, then, is strong, with feeling man coupled with natural (both rational and spiritual) woman. Together, these types can meet social and spiritual crises, as Barbara and Jock have done by the end of the story. This marriage is thoroughly rational. "Ah, Barbara! Barbara!" moans Eunice, "Don't tell me of the Brownings or Charles Kingsley and his wife! Sometimes I am tempted to think that they only had a double lock on their skeleton's closet, and heard the rattle of his dancing all the same. . . . Perfect marriage means the survival of undisturbed devotion through the daily friction of years . . ."(136).

That Amélie Rives had matured greatly as a writer and as a woman is obvious from *Barbara Dering*. Yet, her unhappy marriage—presumably one of the main reasons which caused her to muster such intellectual courage and poise—was worrying her, and that she was able to work at all is surprising. It is less surprising, though, when one notes that the faculties she had developed are characteristic of a strong personality which can exist alone if need be. In 1893, the year after *Barbara Dering* appeared, she published two works, one of which, if it did not surpass the high level of *Barbara Dering*, repeated many of its most mature characteristics.

VI   Tanis, the Sang-Digger (*1893*)

The more vivid of the two works was *Tanis, the Sang-Digger*. It is the story of Tanis Gribble, an uncivilized girl who digs ginseng (or "sang") root for a living. When she first meets George Gilman, a young surveyor who lives near Hot Springs in western Virginia, she wears a dress but not shoes. He finally succeeds in getting her to come home with him so that he can give her some clothes which his wife has cast aside. Tanis, completely candid in her remarks, shocks Alice Gilman by telling her how pale and sickly she looks. A few days later, when Tanis returns to ask the Gilmans if they have any work for her, Alice gives her a job helping the cook; and she learns quickly. Gradually, she comes to respect the refined Gilmans' love for each other and to love Alice as a devoted servant loves a mistress.

Soon, though, her progress in the civilized world is hindered by the appearance of Sam Rose, one of the crude, savage sang-diggers who sleep under the stars in good weather and in one-room hutches in bad and whose only recreations are liquor and free love. He is most anxious to win Tanis as a mistress; and she, being the honest creature she is, freely admits that she loves him, but she also asserts that she now knows love as something more than lust. After she has taken him to the Gilmans' drawing-room window and shown him George reading poetry to Alice, she says she would like a little of this style of love to temper the physical variety. A week later when Rose returns, he admits to staying away from liquor for a week, but he still lusts after Tanis.

She of course refuses to submit, but he catches her in a vulnerable position a few weeks later when she and Alice are riding their horses. On a rough mountain trail Alice's horse trips, throwing her to the ground. When Tanis leaves to get her some water, she returns to find that the horse and Alice have disappeared. When she tells Gilman, he, somewhat dazed, blames her for the incident. A search is launched by Gilman, Tanis, and even by some of the guests at the Homestead, the resort hotel at Hot Springs. A few days later Tanis disappears, but the search continues in vain. Then Tanis suddenly appears at the Homestead one morning and says she knows where Alice is, but that certain promises will have to be made before she will tell. She wants promises that the abductor will not be sought out and that she will not be put in jail.

It turns out that Sam Rose has done the kidnapping and has demanded that Tanis give herself to him as ransom. There is a reconciliation scene in which Gilman begs Tanis to come and live with him and Alice as a daughter; but Tanis cannot do so, for she has made a promise which her simple code of right and wrong will not allow her to break. As she walks slowly up the path from the Homestead toward the hills beyond, an artist living at the hotel says to a friend, "Come here, Davis! Look at that! I swear that's stunning. It would be a good pose for a statue of Eve gazing back at the garden of Eden!"[20] This episode is, of course, supposed to represent the archetypal incident of fallen woman taking her solitary way, leaving behind an Edenic world of innocence and beauty.

Ever at her best in portraying servants and vassals, Amélie made a solid success with Tanis. The dialect is clear and consistent, and the simple soul of the girl makes her tragedy easy to perceive. Reviewers were generally enthusiastic, and those who had been kindly disposed to former works cited usual strong qualities of characterization and accuracy of dialect. Even the detractors, who picked at such negligible features as the plethora of dia-

logue (which exceeds the narrative in volume), appreciated Tanis.
They recognized her as a departure both from the usual Rives
heroine and from other female characters of contemporary fiction
—or, as one reviewer put it, "a devoted and noble savage." [21]

VII   Athelwold: 1893

Athelwold, a drama published the same year, falls short of
Tanis mainly because it is uneven in structure and shows an uncertainty of purpose. These flaws are especially noticeable, as the
basic situation is potentially quite dramatic: the love-honor dilemma so common in Restoration tragedy. The play, however,
takes place in Anglo-Saxon times and has as its protagonist Athelwold, thane and swordsman of King Edgar (959–75). Athelwold
is sent by Edgar to determine the beauty of Elfreda, daughter of
Olgar, Earl of Devonshire. Oswald, an oily priest in Edgar's court,
has told the king of Elfreda's beauty, thinking that Athelwold will
fall in love with her himself and incur the king's wrath; for Oswald is quite jealous of the position which Athelwold occupies in
Edgar's esteem.

Oswald's trap works; Athelwold falls in love with Elfreda and
returns to Edgar with the lie that she is very homely, but that,
being "irked with owing," he might be persuaded to marry her.
When Edgar encourages him to do so, Athelwold returns to Olgar's castle and marries Elfreda. His happiness is short-lived, for
the treachersous Oswald tells the king that he has heard Frothi,
Athelwold's dwarf, talking in his sleep about Elfreda's beauty.
This report plants suspicion in Edgar's mind; and, in a few moments when Athelwold enters the court, he is surprised by the
king's inviting him and Elfreda to dine. Athelwold, who is able to
leave ahead of him, tries to get Elfreda to dress as a hag in order
to disguise her beauty; but she, having never been told of the
king's love, wears her finest clothes and jewels. When Edgar sees
the truth, his first reaction is to hope that she is not really Elfreda,
so high is his regard for Athelwold. But, when he realizes her true
identity, he tells her that it is still not too late for her to become
queen of England. When the king makes this statement, Athelwold draws his sword and fights with him, Edgar wounds him,
and Athelwold dies. When Oswald enters, the dwarf Frothi stabs
him; but, before dying, Oswald asks Edgar to kill Frothi. Edgar

says Frothi will not be punished—that his punishment "is in the hands / Of that High King whom thou [Oswald] hast always served / With more treachery ev'n than thou'st served me, / Thy mortal monarch." [22] The speech and play end with Edgar's simple statement to Athelwold's dead body, "Would to God that I lay there instead of thee!"

There is much about the play that does not ring true to the modern reader: an Anglo-Saxon subject, presented in Elizabethan idiom, shows influences of Restoration tragedy. Such free borrowing was not unusual in the late Victorian period. More often than not, though, the Victorians adapted too freely and with little regard for consistency. The result in *Athelwold* is a patchwork play, not a timeless drama. Although Amélie's sources of the play are unknown, the task of presenting historical fact was obviously more important to her than the exploitation of the tense drama inherent in the situation. For instance, it is clear from the first scene that Athelwold loves his king very much. Yet he sees Elfreda and falls in love with her immediately, without letting loyalty to his ruler halt him. Also, the mood is uneven: in one scene a catastrophe is building, instigated by the fiendish Oswald; the next scene, an idyllic one, shows, for no good reason, Oswald asleep in the forest. Of course, the test of being true either to the facts of a source or to inherent dramatic potential is a pitfall that has trapped many a writer. But *Athelwold* is not a complete failure, for Elfreda and Edgar live as characters; and the blank verse is as good as any the author ever wrote. The play is, however, not another *Herod and Mariamne* in which the protagonist is well motivated and the mood is consistent throughout.

CHAPTER *4*

An End and a Beginning: 1893–1906

DURING most of 1893 the Chanlers remained separated; Amélie traveled as far west as California and as far north as New Hampshire for her health; and he was in Roanoke Rapids, North Carolina, supervising the building of a power station. In the spring of 1894, they sailed for Europe and went first to Paris, as they had on the trip of 1889. This time, however, they were anything but happy newlyweds, and in a few months they separated permanently. By July 4, Amélie was in London alone; the next day she wrote Chanler in Paris regarding their separate properties. There was no bitterness in this or other letters written at this time; apparently both realized that their marriage was a hopeless one.

Later in the summer, Amélie attended a garden party given by Oscar Wilde. A flamboyant affair, it featured singing by the De Reszkes; and many London artistic types were guests. Among this group was Prince Pierre Troubetzkoy, a young portrait artist who had just arrived in England from Milan. Amélie later told her friend Emily Clark Balch that Wilde interrupted her and the Prince, both of whom were talking to other people at the time, and said that they should meet. Legend has it that Wilde thought them the two most beautiful persons present.

Amélie later confided to a friend that it disgusted her to see a beautiful woman give herself to a man who was not equally attractive physically.[1] Pierre's physical appearance must have delighted her. In looking at a drawing which she made in December, 1894, and at a photograph taken by Lord Battersea in the same year, one is immediately struck by Pierre's handsome features and regal bearing. He was likewise her equal in intellect and in artistic accomplishment. Since establishing his studio in "The Boltons," he had painted the portraits of several prominent Englishmen, the most famous of whom was Prime Minister William

[68]

Gladstone. Besides, Pierre's foreign title and his refined social presence made him popular in London social circles.

Soon after meeting Amélie, he painted her portrait,[2] which greatly pleased the cupid-playing Wilde; and soon thereafter, Amélie visited his mother at the Villa Ada, the family home near Pallanza and on the shore of the Lago Maggiore. There she must surely have sensed a romantic atmosphere in which she could feel at home. For Pierre's father, a distant cousin of the Romanovs and married to a close relative of the czar, had fallen in love with Ada Winans, an American opera singer, while on holiday in northern Italy in the 1850's. He had incurred the wrath of the czar, but he was on two occasions given the freedom to return to Russia and be forgiven. He refused, deciding to stay in northern Italy even though it meant forfeiting his wealth and position in Russia. Eventually, his first wife died; and he then married the woman he loved.

In a villa named for the new bride, the Troubetzkoys lived; and in it their three sons were born. Pierre, the eldest, was followed by Paul (the most famous artist of the family) and by Luigi, an engineer and patron of the arts. Though Pierre had studied at the Collegio Calchi Taeggi in Milan, most of his training had come from his own private development of a powerful innate ability. Moreover, he had lived in the midst of some of the most magnificent scenery in the world, and it had engendered an appreciation for vivid color and natural forms. His work is clearly Impressionist, with the typical intensification of detail, and the penchant for building mass by means of short strokes.

Apparently Amélie's acceptance by Princess Ada Troubetzkoy was as immediate as the love between her and the Prince had been. In the autumn she sailed for America; and she was not to see him again until February, 1896, when he came to America for their wedding at Castle Hill. In the meantime, there was the matter of the divorce to settle. Amélie was always concerned that details concerning her marriages be handled with extreme secrecy and discretion. A divorce in those days was the most demanding matter of all. First of all, it was considered a public disgrace and was sensationalized in the case of a person of notoriety. Second, it was a lengthy process. As this was before the days of the "instant divorce," about the best to be hoped for was a six-month decree from far-off South Dakota. This possibility pleased Amélie, as it

meant that she could be out of sight and out of mind. So sometime
in the early spring of 1895, she went to Sioux Falls and began
proceedings which culminated in a final decree in September.
Though the press sided with Chanler and called her "wayward"
and "fickle," both parties were pleased with the terms. Amélie was
given a settlement of thirty-six hundred dollars a year plus one
hundred shares of stock in the Self Threading Sewing Machine
Company, Chanler's latest (and ultimately unsuccessful) business
venture. In return, he received her expressions of interest in his
many projects, addressed to "My own, only *darling* Brother." ³ A
recent commentator is correct in observing that "The divorce accomplished what the marriage could not: they became devoted
friends. . . ." ⁴

They also became neighbors, as Chanler had by this time pur-
chased The Merrie Mills, a plantation located about two miles
from "Amélie's Russian Prince" and his former wife. Here he lived
for forty years, becoming increasingly eccentric and undermining
his fortune by such far-fetched philanthropic schemes as attempting to keep youth on the farms and out of the cities. He died
virtually insane and penniless, but not before he had filled the
press with stories of his bizarre séances, his brilliant escape
from Bloomingdale Asylum, and the much-touted phrase "Who's
looney now?" ⁵

I   *The Princess and* A Damsel Errant (*1898*)

Amélie's marriage to Pierre took place on February 27, 1896, at
Castle Hill with the blessings of John Armstrong Chanler. Shortly
thereafter, the Troubetzkoys sailed for Europe, which, during the
next decade, they visited frequently. Pierre remained busy with
his portraits, and the new Princess revived for a time her own
interest in painting. As a result, her literary creativity suffered;
for, after the publication of *A Damsel Errant* in 1898, she published nothing of consequence until *Seléné,* her only narrative
poem, in 1905.

A *Damsel Errant* is important only because it represents the
end of an important period of her artistic development. Published
as part of Lippincott's "Lotus Library," it took its place beside
such negligible romances as Julian Hawthorne's *The Golden
Fleece* and Robert Buchanan's *A Marriage by Capture.* It carried

an advertisement which boasted that "the wonderful works of this authoress" had made a deeper impression on American letters than any work except *Uncle Tom's Cabin*. A brief look at the plot shows how *A Damsel Errant* appealed to the same popular mind that had admired the Uncle Tom melodrama.

The setting in fifteenth-century France was especially attractive to popular taste. It offered the same lure of the long ago and far away as "A Brother to Dragons," and it also rewarded the reader with a story of a lord and lady in love. The latter attraction features Loys de Vallon and Yovanne, only daughter of the aged Baron de Savare. The tomboyish Yovanne is introduced as a man hater, and she rejects the suits of all comers including that of Loys, even though he twice saves her life early in the story. Shortly after his rejection, Loys and the old Baron accidentally meet, argue, and duel. The Baron falls on his sword and is killed, and Loys is taken to prison; but, of course, Yovanne arrives in time to save him from execution.

Romances usually require suspension of the reader's disbelief and demand acceptance of the unreal and the improbable, but even the most indulgent reader balks at some of the glaring impositions of this narrative. Amélie, apparently unsure of her direction when she began, has Loys narrate the first two-thirds of the story; and she then brings in a hitherto unknown page to complete the job when Loys is taken to prison. A more glaring instance of disjointedness concerns Yovanne's intercession for Loys's life. It is not enough that her feelings for him have run, unmotivated, from rejection, to a belief that he has killed her father, and then to ardent love. Nor is it sufficient to have a Spanish dwarf witness from a tree the death of the Baron, then fall and knock himself unconscious, and finally awaken in time to testify that the old man has died accidentally and not by Loys's sword. But at the crucial moment when Loys is on the gallows, the suddenly loving Yovanne runs in, ignores the dwarf's evidence altogether, and unexpectedly produces an ancient Norman law which offers freedom to a condemned man if he has an offer of marriage from an eligible woman.

When all she needed to do was to offer the dwarf's testimony of Loys's innocence, Yovanne's grandstand gesture seems rather like scene stealing. One of the more unsympathetic of the Rives heroines, she is no credit to the genre of popular Romance and much

less to the first period of her creator's work. In the absence of a
dated manuscript or other more conclusive evidence, one can only
guess that *A Damsel Errant* must have been written in the late
1880's while Amélie was writing other fiction set in the Middle
Ages. Otherwise, it is difficult to comprehend how the talent that
produced *Barbara Dering* could have regressed this far.

II   *A Period of Silence: 1898–1905*

Just after Amélie's marriage to Prince Troubetzkoy, a young
free-lance writer named Willa Cather sneeringly observed, "So
Amélie Rives is married again and to a Russian Prince. Princess
Troubetzkoy, that will look well under the title of her next sensational novel. . . ." [6] This was indeed the era when new American
fortunes were frequently exchanged for old European titles across
the marriage altar. Henry James had written of numerous encoun-
ters between culturally shabby Americans, lured by ancient traditions, and European nobility; and H. L. Mencken later spoke of
"perfumed Italians coming over to work their abominable magic
on the daughters of breakfast-food and bathtub kings. . . ." [7]

That Amélie Rives took pride in her new title there is little
doubt. On her books and in her correspondence, it invariably followed her maiden name. Such, however, is a superfluous gesture
which in no way detracts from the weightier facts of emotional
happiness and artistic development. The title which came with
her marriage was really incidental to Amélie, whose sense of personal identity was already secure.

The same was true of Pierre. Unlike Chanler, who had pursued
his own selfish interests at the cost of neglecting those of his wife,
Pierre shared an artistic interest with Amélie which had the effect
of sustaining her as never before. She, in turn, was proud of his
talents and achievements and regarded various aspects of both as
superior to her own. Pierre was not able to enjoy this symbiotic
relationship without some sacrifices, however. He had wanted to
paint as a purely creative artist; and, had he been able to do so, he
might have rivaled the success of his brother Paul, whose sculp-
ture is prominently displayed throughout Europe. Instead, he
willingly elected to paint portraits to help support the woman he
loved. This selfless gesture was one of which Chanler would have
never been capable.

The gentle side of the Prince's nature was appreciated by virtually everyone with whom he came into contact. Emily Clark thought him "really . . . too nice to be an artist." [8] The Castle Hill servants, who called him "Mister Prince," loved him dearly. He possessed a childlike innocence which impressed many people, sometimes in the wrong way. The story is often told of his walking about the front lawn of Castle Hill barefoot, as he was wont to do, during the period in the early 1930's when Amélie and her sister Landon had opened the house to visitors. When, up the long box-wood-lined drive, a large car appeared, bearing an elegantly dressed woman, the barefoot figure walked over to her, introduced himself as Prince Troubetzkoy, and awaited her name, which was Katharine Hepburn. With true candor, his first question was, "And what do you do, Miss Hepburn?" On the other hand, he had courtly manners and donned a white tie for dinner each evening. Quite unconsciously, in interviewing people who knew him, one notes the invariable reference, "The Prince."

But it was his artistic ability and not his title which gained him commissions to paint members of the Vanderbilt, Du Pont, Astor, and Roosevelt families. In addition, he continued to paint portraits abroad until the outbreak of World War I. Summers were spent in the guest house of the Villa Ada near Pallanza, and winters in New York. In between, he and Amélie stayed at Castle Hill, where he had a studio and easy access to Richmond, which furnished him many commissions.

Although little is known of Amélie's life during the early years of her marriage to Pierre, it seems safe to infer that she thrived upon his emotional and intellectual companionship. In the decade before her marriage, she had emerged from a secure position as private citizen into public controversy and partnership in a shaky marriage which had ended in divorce. In retrospect, her work during this period was quite uneven, ranging from the jejune *According to St. John* to the masterful *Barbara Dering*. And, while it is true that *Barbara Dering* was written during the most crisis-ridden of these years and represents a triumph of spirit and mind over formidable matter, its high quality is still as much an exception as the display of effort it called forth. The work of the second period—1905 to 1938—was of a more consistent quality. Few of the earlier faults were repeated, and on balance it far surpassed the earlier period. It seems certain, therefore, that the security

and intellectual stimulation offered by the marriage was a major
contributing factor.

III   Seléné (1905)

Seléné, the first work of the new period, and the first book-
length work since *A Damsel Errant,* set the precedent for Amélie's
works of the second period. It was the author's first attempt at
narrative poetry, her first use of Greek myths, and her first and
only work written in the Esthete mode. It is a harbinger of the
new themes, genres, and settings which were to follow.

Some orientation is necessary for a proper understanding of
Seléné, not only because legends about the subject vary, but also
because Amélie adapted them rather freely. Moreover, Seléné has
more than one identity in the poem. At times she is Diana, or
Artemis, the chaste huntress. At others, she is Phoebe, or Seléné,
the moon goddess (twin of Phoebus Apollo, the sun god). Both
she and Phoebus are the issue of Zeus and Leto, one of his many
mortal amours. Though Themis (Zeus's wife before Hera) resents
the twins, she develops such an affection for Phoebus that she
prophesies only future good for him. For Seléné, however, she
prophesies undefined misfortune which could be averted only if
she remained neutral toward love. If, however, she became either
love's friend or foe, she would reap unhappiness.

Seléné has been able to maintain neutrality until just before the
beginning of the poem. In the guise of Diana the huntress, she has
recently followed her hounds, who track a doe to a mysterious
cave. There she has found a beautiful young man asleep, who
resembles Apollo more than she herself does. For the first time the
chaste huntress surrenders to impulse and kisses the young man
on the eyes and forehead. The first scene of the poem shows her
telling these events to her former nurse, Steropé, and asking for
her advice.

Steropé is concerned over the well-being of her former charge.
She has learned, however, that Hera, the present wife of Zeus, has
set this trap for her husband's bastard daughter's disaster. Moreover, Steropé has formerly loved a mortal; and, as a result, she,
who had been the seventh pleiade, is now virtually invisible. Instead of being grateful for Steropé's advice, Seléné becomes de-
fensive and asserts that she is, after all, a goddess (which is half

right) and is not afraid to confront Eros himself. When Steropé chides her for her arrogance, Seléné counters by reminding Steropé of her fallen state.

The scene then shifts to the Carian prince Endymion who, having fared badly in love, has been dreaming of a pleasant life devoid of it. Somewhat like Amélie, "He had known / The sapping, slow, brain-sucking misery / That falls upon the passionate whom error / Unto the passionless hath bound. . . ." [9] Now, however, his passion has turned to the moon, which he has come to worship.

Seléné now invokes Eros, something which no mortal ever dares to do. He comes disguised to human eyes as a swan, but Seléné can see him in a boat of thinnest ivory. He is described in the most sensual of imagery, which is as extreme in this regard as any of the *fin de siècle* "Esthetes'" work:

> A crown of jonquils intertwined with stars
> Rested above his dark and tender brows,
> Wherein was gathered all the mystic gloom
> That haunts the far, faint level of the sea.
> Yearning his eyes, as of a soul bereft
> Beyond what to mortals or immortals
> Is of bereavement known, yet on his lips
> That listless smile, more deadly sweet than cold
> Than frozen honey culled from poisonous flowers,
> Still palely wavered. From one indolent hand
> There hung a torch of mother-pearl, whose flames
> Lilac and topaz-white and violet azure,
> Clustered in petal-wise about the centre,
> Till like a clear-blue lotus-flower they seemed;
> Nor robe nor mantle wore he, being clad
> In his own splendour as in golden gauze,
> Wherethrough his languid limbs gleamed silverly,
> Veiled yet hidden not. . . . (50)

When Seléné asks Eros to vow that he and she may forever be neither friend nor foe, he asserts this state cannot exist, for anyone who beholds him must be either one or the other. Moreover, he reminds her that she is half human, as her pride indicates. She finds his argument distasteful, thinking his powerful love odious in contrast to the chastity she represents. He corrects her by telling her that "Chastity is not abstinence, but temperance. / True chastity is truer for true love. / Negative purity white pebbles

have, / Being cold and white, even as thou art, Seléné, / Who art
not chaste because of conquered fire, / But merely chill, bearing a
heart unkindled"(58). He then asserts that he is badly misunder-
stood—that he is "the mirror of the universe"(61). If men of
heavenly natures look upon him, they see the heavenly; if earthly,
the common. He says that Steropé is a good example of this fact,
having been overcome with love for an earthling. However, Eros
declares that worship of him enhances human life.

Seléné still refuses to take what he says seriously; instead, she
believes that he is double-talking. But he implores her to accept
his friendship by arguing: "Then, Artemis, thou shalt possess /
Greater by far than Hera's hair of gold; / A kingdom such as Zeus
hath never swayed; / A height of vast immaculate repose / Where-
from Olympos, viewed, will seem a mound / Of marble-dust by
children heaped in play . . ."(68). Seléné's reply is to grab one of
her arrows and drive it into her breast in an attempt to kill herself.
But she soon finds that Moera, or Fate (who, along with Love and
Death, rules the universe), has replaced one of her arrows with
one belonging to Eros; and she now has no alternative but to become his friend. So great a thirst does this wound give her that she
can only slake it by drinking the wine of Fate (symbolizing, of
course, commitment to whatever Fate may lead her into). Suddenly, she is no longer able to see Eros in all his magnificence; he
has now become veiled. When she blindly asks forgiveness for
having scoffed at him, he grants it; however, he warns that she
will have to suffer for her scoffing before she can see him in his
glory again. Nevertheless, he reassures her that "Whom I befriend
/ Are by all gods befriended at the last" (79). So Seléné, drinking
the wine of Fate, is drawn to love and exits, calling "Endymion, I
come!"(82).

From an autobiographical point of view, this poem is most important. One could scarcely avoid investigating the fascination
which this of all subjects should have held for the Princess at this
time as a close parallel to her own life. Seléné is, after all, an
Edenic character; and this story tells of her loss of innocence in
love and of her gaining knowledge of both good and evil in passionate love. The fact that Seléné's choice is directed by Fate is
unimportant; what is significant is that she is inevitably drawn
into a realm of love that is deeper and more complex than she
could have conceived as existing in her former state of chastity.

The author may well have seen herself, in retrospect, as a prideful young woman who was now involved in a love to the fate of which she had given herself completely. It may well have been that she now realized that this love was her only way to true happiness, even though it meant a loss of the naïve Romanticism seen in her early stories.

Also, it is only natural that this rarefied subject should have attracted many readers at the beginning of this century. Any reader who could read and appreciate an Esthete like Oscar Wilde or Ernest Dowson could certainly find pleasure in this sensual love poem whose sole object was to take love from its pedestal and give it currency by making it more vivid. The description of Eros (quoted above) is absolutely decadent in spots and might well have been sung to Cynara, Salome, Yvonne of Brittany, or any of the other heroines of Esthete poetry. Still, Amélie really belonged to no particular "school," for she wrote about what fascinated her most; but her tastes were somewhat shaped by the times; and this poem is a fine example. It shows, however, that, while this poem resembles the work of those English poets whose Bohemian lives were every bit as decadent as their verse, it was written by a lady of much sophistication and discretion. Moreover, it shows that she was of strong enough mind to withstand the floodtide of Naturalism. While readers of this generation were suffering with the protagonists of Stephen Crane, Frank Norris, and Theodore Dreiser as they fought against a Darwinistic environment, Amélie chose to create the esoteric air of Attic hillsides and to evince her highly developed sense of individualism and discriminating taste.

It is unfortunate that her lack of sound criticism of her own work should have led her away from writing narrative poetry. Her only other volume of poetry was *As the Wind Blew,* a collection of lyrics published in 1922, many of which had appeared in magazines or incidentally in novels. On the whole, this volume is inferior to *Seléné,* for there is a flabbiness and vagueness in many of the lyrics not found in this poem.

IV   Augustine the Man (*1906*)

The finely wrought blank verse which had characterized *Seléné* became the following year a salient feature of *Augustine the Man.*

Amélie always considered this drama her highest achievement, and its poetry gives good reason for her so considering it. Her assessment was doubtlessly prompted by certain personal factors, however, such as a love for Milan and the lake region of northern Italy and a sympathy for anyone forced to grapple with soul-searching dilemmas.

The theme of the play is the spiritual growth of Augustine, one which can be plotted by the four geographic areas in which the scenes are laid: his severest doubts in Carthage; his conversion in Milan; his life as a monk in the Villa Verecundas on the Lago Maggiore; and, finally, the death of his illegitimate son Adeodatus in Tagaste, Augustine's birthplace. In the first scene, Augustine is living in Carthage with Melcara, his mistress of many years and their son, Adeodatus. Though undergoing great spiritual turmoil, Augustine is still not very much troubled about his sensuality. He has just finished a series of debates with Faustus, the Manichaean philosopher; and, though he has become disaffected with this philosophy, he is by no means ready to accept Christianity, which would preclude the sensuality he has been practicing. But the chief obstacle between Augustine and Christianity is also his reason for rejecting the Manichaean beliefs: his own intellectual conclusions; for he has realized the shallowness of Faustus's arguments, and this realization turns him away from his beliefs. Yet he is unable to reconcile Christianity to his intellect, though he can basically accept it in his heart: "While my heart acclaims him [Christ], / My reason questions. . . ." [10] He is in need of intellectual satisfaction, however, for he exclaims, "I am weary / With seeking God as mariners, oft shipwrecked, / Are weary of the sea, yet cannot long / Abide beyond the terror of its voice" (29).

One of the greatest obstacles Augustine faces is the refusal of his exalted intelligence to accept a shallow concept of God. This view is implicit not only in his struggles in the first scene but also after his conversion when he finds that he has accepted a God who is not always benign and who is at times cruel beyond belief. Melcara, in her untutored wisdom, tells him of "Melcarth the beautiful, who loved not blood" (11); but he realizes that this pagan Carthaginian deity (for whom she is named) is an oversimplification of the God he has been able to sense only in his heart. In order to be able to accept God rationally, Augustine must understand a God who might very well be sorry that He

created man because of his sorrow over man's sufferings, which
He has also created. Since Augustine realizes that God has also
created Satan, his problem lies in reconciling a being whose complexities are overwhelming.

Also, Augustine is portrayed as a man who has tasted fully of
life and who has left nothing to innocent acceptance—a vivid contrast to Antonius, a devout, if somewhat shallow and conventional
Christian:

> Thou hast not thought thyself kinsman to God,
> Yet stooped thy high estate to cherish demons.
> Thou hast not thought the fire divine burned in thee
> And used it but to light the torch of lust.
> Thou hast not cried "Truth! Truth!" and lived but lies.
> Thou hast not searched the universe for God,
> And found thine own dire self was god to thee! . . . (19–20)

Yet Antonius well realizes Augustine's problem: "Thy mind is like
a mirror swung in space, / And whirling on a thread. Now it re-
flecteth / The heavens, and now the earth . . ."(28).

In the second scene, which takes place in Milan, Augustine is
still looking for a way to "re-beget" himself and to "die unto life."
This is most difficult for him to do, not only because of his sensuality, but because of pride in his own intellect. After a passionate
entreaty to God to "Grant that this cup which I myself have
brimmed / With loathliness, pass from me! . . ." (46), he hears a
voice which says "Tolle . . . lege" (Take, read); and he remembers the reading which he and his old friend Alypius have been
doing earlier in the afternoon. He goes to the Bible which Alypius
has left open and reads from Romans XIII:13–14: "Not in rioting
and drunkenness, not in chambering and wantonness, not in strife
and envying: but put ye on the Lord Jesus Christ, and make not
provision for the flesh, to fulfill the lusts thereof" (48). "All my
night is day!," he exclaims; and the scene ends.

The next scene shows his separation from Melcara, who cannot
accept his conversion as a wise one; for she believes Christ to be a
much harsher God than Melcarth, "who loves not blood." Augustine's mother, Monica, prays for Melcara; and, in the end, Augustine prays both for himself and for the woman he deeply loves. In
the final two scenes, which concern the outcome of Augustine's
decision, Adeodatus tells him of having scourged himself after

hearing a young Roman poet sing of sensual subjects. At the end of the scene the poet actually appears on the stage, symbolizing Augustine's memory of his former life of the flesh. The final scene shows the death of Adeodatus, and Augustine's words show even then the torture in his soul: "Oh, poor Melcara! How art thou avenged! / Thinking but of myself I took him from thee"(83). This declaration is the final indication that Augustine's God is anything but an easy God to serve and that, even though Augustine has physically rejected the flesh and embraced the spirit, he still suffers as a mortal.

Both because of its poetry and of the vividly depicted pathos of Augustine's conscience, the drama deserves praise as a distinguished accomplishment—but not the unqualified praise which its author bestowed upon it. For, judged in terms of dramatic structure, several important ground rules have been violated. First, the exposition usually expected in the opening scenes of a play is almost nonexistent; and one would have to be familiar with the life of Augustine to understand or appreciate the action and character motivation. Second, there is virtually no organic evolution from scene to scene: one never knows, for example, what causes Augustine to go from Carthage to Milan. Third, there is no accounting for what happens to Melcara, one of the most sympathetic characters in the play. The fault of being true to history rather than to art is quite evident, just as it had been in *Athelwold*. In language and language alone the story lives as art as opposed to history.

If, however, one assumes that the play is meant to be purely poetry, some of these faults can be overlooked. For then one can appreciate the production primarily for its language and forget about its weaknesses as a possible stage production or even as a closet drama. It could well have been intended primarily as poetry, for how else could Adeodatus's stage direction, *"Dreamily, a look of his mother coming over his face,"* have any meaning? One is still left, however, with the lack of motivation and structure which in closet or stage drama is a primary requirement.

CHAPTER *5*

From the Summit: 1908–45

IN THE same article of 1894 that sneered at Amélie Rives's marriage to Prince Troubetzkoy and aimed vitriolic barbs at her early work, Willa Cather observed that the Princess had tried to write a "literature of passion", which, she added, is "the most difficult sort of fiction in the world." In Miss Cather's opinion, she wrote it "passing poorly." "The literature of passion is either very great art or very great rot," she continued. "When it is subjective, it is usually the latter." [1]

It is understandable that Miss Cather should have found fault with this "literature of passion" since she spent an entire career producing a literature of tight restraint. She held no monopoly on this realm of literature, however; and, had she written a corresponding assessment at the end of Amélie's second artistic period, she would have been forced to concede—grudgingly, one supposes—that Amélie had likewise earned citizenship. *Seléné* and *Augustine the Man* had shown both increased control and decreased subjectivity over the first period. Both concerned initiations—Seléné, into love; Augustine, into religion. That the author could speak with such detached authority of the trials involved in each case and that she so well understood the complexities of either state indicate that she too had become additionally experienced in the realities of her art in particular and of human experience in general. Her deepened understanding of reality made her less prone to treat her subject matter with the old subjectivity that Miss Cather had deplored. She now approached her material more dispassionately and probed it with more of a scientific disinterestedness.

This is not to say, however, that Amélie abandoned the topics which had attracted her interest in the early period. She still wrote of sensitive heroines struggling in love affairs with insensitive males. Now more than ever, she was drawn to situations in-

volving the conflict and ultimate triumph of the human spirit.
These themes may well be transformed into an unbridled literature of passion, but not if the author is wary and skillful enough to
control them. *The Golden Rose* is the first work of the second
period to show that Amélie's abilities had developed to the point
of viewing a hypersensitive heroine's love affair with objectivity
and of projecting it into a novel with restraint.

I The Golden Rose (1908)

For the first few pages, *The Golden Rose* promises more of the
first period's weaknesses. Meraud Cabell, the heroine, goes about
making such statements as "I am love! . . . the great love, the
true love, the love for all that is, the love that is real. The other is
all Maya—all illusion." [2] Just divorced from a "libertine cousin,"
she rebounds with a zest typical of her Rivesian ancestors: "I'm
like a rose cut back to the roots," she says. "I'm all fresh little twigs
and leaves and buds . . ."(9).

Obviously, this first chapter is charged with the old unbridled
emotion. Meraud and her friend Anice Mayo frequently fall on
each other with kisses. (Mercifully, they are not subjected to
Freudian criticism in these pages.) Yet, this chapter, for all its
fawning, presents a sharp insight into character and theme. The
theme concerns two kinds of love: the sort practiced by most men
(which Meraud calls "hunger") and the ideal kind visualized by
Meraud (which she calls "thirst," and which is as close to a Platonic abstraction as one could expect to get). This Platonic love
makes Meraud a "strange soul"—strange in the sense that she is
able to live in the realm of the spirit, which is something the average individual does but seldom—if at all. Much of her conversation reflects her knowledge of Eastern philosophies such as the
Bhagavad-Gita and Yoga. All this sounds esoteric, of course, yet
such is not the case after the first chapter; for this atmosphere is
cleverly counterbalanced by means of such foils as the down-to-
earth Dr. Dundas, whose observations brim with common sense.
Moreover, the setting is Kingsweather, another copy of the Castle
Hill prototype, and is located near Charlottesville. Thus the story
is given sufficient Realism to offset the ethereality of Meraud's
concept of love. Finally, Meraud herself is shown as part of a

recognizable society, so that her spiritual and physical sides are at all times separately discernible.

Just before the end of the first chapter, Stephen Gordon Trafford is introduced into the story. He is a young historian and a kinsman of a professor at the university in nearby Charlottesville. Trafford, who is writing a history of that region of Virginia, has heard that Meraud has some manuscripts which she might be willing to show him. She consents to do so; invites him to have lunch; and then, because of a rising storm, invites him to stay the night. He is immediately struck by her beauty; but, since he has heard a great deal about her attitude toward men, he does not reveal his feelings. Still, during the storm (always in the Princess' work a time for truth and frankness), he and Meraud discuss freely their feelings about storms; and, from this exchange, they establish a rapport based upon their similarity of reactions.

During the next few days, as Trafford works with the manuscripts, the friendship grows; but he makes every effort to repress the romantic fancies which naturally arise. Meraud, in the meantime, while admitting she likes Trafford but still unchanged in her attitude toward love, decides to ask him to spend a few weeks at Kingsweather. During his stay Dr. Dundas, an old friend of the family, visits Meraud on his way to New York; for he has been quite concerned about her nervous condition after the divorce. As one of the touchstones of Realism in the book, he is quick to see that Trafford is in love with his hostess and that she may very well return his affection. He tells Anice that he has inquired about Trafford and has found that, while an admirable individual, he would not make a good husband for Meraud because there is "not enough to him"(125).

Trafford soon expresses his love, but Meraud tells him that she could never marry again. He tells her that he is not after the "marrying kind of love," and both seem satisfied with this arrangement. During the next several weeks, they walk, read, and ride together; and both seem perfectly happy. When she tells him that he has helped her to experience her highest ideal of love, she quotes Genevieve, a friend of hers who had died uttering "Always the painted apple, never the golden rose"(155)—a line which represents the friend's futility in finding happiness in love and one which also points to the theme of the story. Meraud tells Trafford that he has given her the golden rose, or the ideal love; but it soon becomes evident that she has been the only one to feel this emotion, for the feeling which Trafford has more resembles the "painted apple."

This duality is cleverly woven into the story in a number of ways. During one of their early walks, Meraud, who has been discussing the fireflies flitting around them, remarks that one of them, flying higher than the others, must think himself a star; and Trafford answers that more than likely he thinks some star a firefly (80). Later in the story, when Trafford is about to leave on his journey, the two stand before an old moon dial, which contains the Latin quotation *Ad astra per aspira,* which for her is eventually to have the proper meaning, "to the stars through aspiration," while for him it is to have exactly the opposite significance.

Their "ideal" love continues, and one begins to wonder how long it can last or how it will finally resolve itself when Trafford gets a letter from a friend whom he has promised to accompany on a trip to India. By now he, of course, hates to go; but Meraud encourages him to do so, believing, in John Donne fashion, that their souls will remain as one even though physically separated. Much of this scene takes place by the moon dial with its inscription, which is soon to prove a *double-entendre.*

For the first few weeks that Trafford is away, he writes every day, as does she. During this time, though, he is sustained by the fresh memory of her physical presence. Then comes a point when he enters that part of India where the mail is irregular, so for several weeks she receives no letter. When one finally arrives, she locks herself in her room to read it, only to find the old warmth gone and the tone rather cold; and his succeeding letters are much the same. Finally, he writes that he has been injured in a fall and has received poor medical treatment; but he has sufficiently recovered to meet her in New York in a few days. She goes to New York to meet him, and they accidentally meet in a rather tawdry theater (obviously intended to represent the commonplace character of his love and, by contrast, the nobility of hers). He seems embarrassed at first and tells her apologetically that he will see her the next day. He does so; and, though they spend many hours together, Meraud is quite sure that the spark of their relationship has gone out. His love has been the painted apple, which has been unable to sustain the burden of physical removal, while hers, the golden rose, has endured.

She returns to Virginia, having told Trafford that she doesn't think they should see each other for a year. For all practical purposes the affair is over, however. When she arrives back at Kingsweather, Anice summons Dr. Dundas. He is confident that, because of her great depth of spirit, Meraud will recover from the hurt she has sustained. Doctor Dundas observes:

> She will find happiness in being able to set aside happiness, and yet remain herself—unshaken—sweet to the core. She is like one of those springs of fresh water that rise sometimes in the sea. . . . She dared to use wings, We all know what happened to Icarus. "Serves him right." Melted wax and a breakneck fall, that's what *his* ideal ended in! But she falls up. Her wings aren't waxed on; they are rooted in her life. A wind has blown her off her course, beyond her present goal. That's all. There are bigger things in store for that soul than the love of just one for just one. (216)

The last scene shows Meraud walking among the surroundings which she and Trafford had known—even by the moon dial with the inscription of which she does not yet know the full meaning. She thinks to herself that love can never be recovered, and she realizes the limitations of Trafford's capacity to love. At the very end of the story, she pictures herself as an old woman who bears the painted apple in her hand and who toils along "the ancient, narrow path—as hard to tread as the edge of a razor"(226). This ending is a thoroughly satisfactory one, for the painted apple, representing Trafford's love, still burdens her mind; but the image of the razor's edge, taken from the Hindu *Upanishads* and used throughout the novel to describe the excruciating steps toward self-fulfillment, clearly indicates that her recent ordeal is but another step in her pilgrimage.

One is reminded of the final scenes of Hawthorne's story "The Artist of the Beautiful," one of his seldom acknowledged masterpieces. Owen Warland, the "artist," has created his masterpiece, a butterfly that will fly and alight like the real insect. At the end of the story the marvelous invention is seized and crushed by the son of the woman he has forsaken for his art. All who see the incident are shocked and deeply concerned, but not Owen Warland: "He had caught a far other butterfly than this. When the artist rose high enough to achieve the beautiful, the symbol by which he made it perceptible to mortal senses became of little value in his eyes while his spirit possessed itself in the enjoyment of reality." [3] Meraud has experienced the golden rose, something which few have done. The physical relationship which made it possible, like Warland's butterfly, has been destroyed. Yet "her spirit possessed itself in the enjoyment of the reality" even though it was past.

Despite the fact that the love theme is the most potentially sentimental of subjects, the author is notably rigorous in both her attitude toward the subject and in the language itself. The rigor of treatment seen in *Barbara Dering* and the explicitness of language found in *Seléné* and in *Augustine the Man* have come together to make this unquestionably the best novel since *Barbara Dering*, which had appeared sixteen years before. Another area of strength derives from an extended use of point of view, which is limited omniscient. The main value of this innovation is an increased awareness of character motivation, something which has been sorely lacking before. This angle of narration also means that there is less need for the "teller" to appear in the story and that intrinsic elements of the story can be utilized to a greater degree.

A final area of interest is autobiography. Meraud possesses many characteristics which resemble those of the mature Princess. For example, she is able to project her mind to distant places and to tell what is happening there. Moreover, in the end of the book she is able to call cardinals to her. The Princess claimed to be able to perform both these feats, and living witnesses attest to her success. More importantly, though, one can see in Meraud a close parallel to the author's emotional maturity. From the vivacious Virginia Herrick in "Virginia of Virginia," through the sensitive Ilva Demarini in *Witness of the Sun*, through the fiery intellectualism of *Barbara Dering*, the development has followed a regular progression to the mature woman—the woman seen in many of the succeeding novels—whose eclectic reading, combined with a keen sensitivity, has made it possible to attain the ideal love that Barbara Dering never really learned how to achieve. In the final analysis, what Barbara had learned was reconciliation; but Meraud achieves the fulfillment of an ideal without making any

such compromise, as the Princess herself had apparently done by
now.

II   Trix and Over-the-Moon (*1909*)

For all the interest that parallels between heroine and author
may hold for the reader, it is refreshing to note that the protagonist of *Trix and Over-the-Moon* is modeled upon someone else.
Beatrix ("Trix") Bruce is obviously based upon the Princess' older
sister Gertrude who had married Colonel Tom Potts and had
moved to the nearby plantation Happy Creek. Here she was able
to give a great deal of time to her three favorite pastimes: her
garden, her horses, and her hound pack. She became the most
famous equestrienne Virginia ever produced and was for a time
the only female Master of Hounds in the nation. Though she was
not particularly close to the Princess, this book was dedicated to
her "with love."

While Trix's only literary bent is a knowledge of Horace, whom
she is always quoting, she nevertheless has a quick wit and a
sharp eye. She uses these capacities for running the plantation
while her husband, Sidney Nelson Bruce, stays in his study and
writes sentimental novels (Colonel Potts was a journalist). The
first part of the story concerns the purchase of a colt sired by
Orion, which she names "Over-the-Moon," after realizing what a
fine steeplechaser he will make. She is overjoyed with her purchase; but Joe Scott, her trainer, has misgivings. He believes the
horse to have a mean streak, as do all the offspring of Orion. And
Trix has more trials than usual training him: sometimes he goes
down on his knees and throws her; at others, he refuses to take a
hurdle. Yet she insists that she is going to show him in the fall, and
nothing her husband or Joe can say dissuades her, even though
she realizes by now that she is expecting another baby.

At this point in the narrative, Alison Stark, who has been "nan-
nie" both to Sidney and Tim, the Bruces' son, begins an elaborate
scheme to save Trix and the unborn child. At first she uses all the
powers of her persuasive Scottish eloquence to stop Trix, but is
unsuccessful. As in all other instances, Trix is a headstrong woman
who will not be told what to do even by her husband. So she
kindly but firmly refuses to listen to Alison, telling her that she

knows enough about horses not to get hurt. Alison then tries a new tactic: she begins to make friends with the animal. She feeds him sugar and soon gets him to come at her whistle. This wooing continues through the summer, as time for the horse shows approaches.

One of the most interesting sidelights in the story is the argument between Alison and "Mammy Henny," Trix's old Negro servant. These two are typically brilliant low-character portrayals. Both the Negro and Scottish dialects are flawless, and the many arguments between the two call forth a broad stream of each. Both agree, however, that Trix will be in trouble if she persists in taking the horse to the shows. So after Alison has completely won the horse's confidence, she calls Mammy Henny to her room one day and gives her a beautiful black silk gown and a brooch, gifts which thrill her. Then she gives Trix some dainty clothes for the new baby. She even gives little Tim a gold dollar, and gets him to promise that when she has gone to Scotland, he will tell his parents of the whereabouts of some envelopes (which contain, unknown to him, gifts for all the Negroes on the plantation).

That night Alison puts some scant belongings in a tartan and goes to the stall of Over-the-Moon. One of the items she has brought along is a knife; and, while she feeds him sugar, she severs his jugular vein. When she leaves, she has left behind half of her life savings to pay for the horse and a letter explaining why she has done the deed. She is found; is brought back to Oldwood; and, in an ending reminiscent of the Princess' fictional worst, dies —but not before receiving forgiveness from "Maister Seedney," who, of course, returns from a New York trip just in time.

Though contrived and sentimental, this ending should be taken to indicate not the failure of the whole book, but a general unevenness. The first half contains some of the surest pages of narrative that the Princess ever wrote. There is an ease in the style and the exposition of facts, and there is a charm in the depiction of life on a Virginia plantation early in the twentieth century; and the proper focus is placed upon Trix and the horse. Then, almost exactly halfway through the novel, Alison Stark is introduced. While quaint and picturesque with her Scottish brogue and her loyalty to her "maister," she seems to assume the center of interest. The changeover is awkward: one is left with the tragedy of Alison

Stark, after having been led to expect the exciting life of Beatrix Bruce.

There are some surprising artistic touches, such as the stream-of-subconsciousness passage in which Trix's mind is turning over the possibility of starting a hound pack as she sews on a gown for the Richmond German.[4] This picture is a perfect one of Trix, for she is athletic, yet likes to make at least an attempt at being domestic. What she considers to be her chef-d'œuvre of interior decoration is a massive brass bed with its connecting rivets exposed. Yet, when Sidney reads her a passage from one of his sentimental novels, she is able to deflate it in short order by saying "*Just* be natural . . . *just* be easy . . . *just* be simple. You used to be all three . . . before you decided you had a career[. . . .] You're just praying to Fame and staring at your own eyes in a glass all the time, Sidney. That's what's the matter with you. . . . That's why you don't like your own books . . . and that's why people won't buy 'em[. . .] (47). She calls his heroines "[un]like anyone in the heavens above or the earth beneath or the waters under the earth. . . . At least, not like anyone *I* ever saw . . ." (47–48). Such cannot be said of Trix, however; for she is in every sense alive and at times seems to be larger than life. Since Trix is the intended center of interest in the story, it is appropriate that half of it is narrated from her point of view; however, the novel is flawed by the uneven plot and by the shift in emphasis from Trix to Alison.

III   Pan's Mountain (*1910*)

By 1910, the Troubetzkoys had made numerous trips back to the lake region of Italy, an area which has deserved the acclaim it has been given. To the Romanticist, it furnishes an infinite amount of opportunity to stretch the imagination and to let the fancy roam. From the Villa Ada, one can look straight across the icy blue waters toward Stresa; looking northward, he can see the snowy caps of the Swiss Alps. One can easily sense the superstition of the simple folk of the region, who are far more Germanic than Mediterranean. The impact that this romantic, mystical land and its people made upon the Princess is easily visible in *Pan's Mountain*. Doubtlessly, the Alps reminded her of her distant Blue

Ridge country, for the robust, natural heroine who had inhabited that region in so many of her novels is much at home in the setting of this one.

Dione Rupin has been named by her Russian-born father in honor of Aether and Ge, the two gods who rule the earth and sky. Her father's teachings that such deities rule the universe and not the Catholic hierarchy has caused her to live in close touch with her natural environment. He taught her as he did in order that she might have an objective view of religion and not the Catholic slant which her mother had wished. Dione has learned her lessons well, for she reflects little of orthodox Italian society, or of any conventional society for that matter. Moreover, her old nursemaid, Cecca, has helped nurture her free, pagan existence. Cecca, who lives in a small cottage behind the Rupin villa, is so superstitious that she makes the sign of horns to ward off evil every time something resembling the supernatural is mentioned.

Dione's father had died when she was fourteen; and now, at eighteen, she still lives with her rather shallow, conventional mother whose fondest hope is that Dione will find a wealthy husband. A logical candidate is young Gigino Varoni, who lives close by. He has loved Dione for a long time, but she finds him a bore. She seems to be waiting for a special mate, the kind suggested by her recent visit to the Sasso di Ferro (Mountain of Iron, which she calls "Pan's Mountain"). Here she has poured a libation of wine onto the earth at the base and asked Pan to "Bring home my mate to me from among all other men, and grant that our sons be strong and wise." [5]

Though Gigino does not fulfill this expectation, it soon becomes obvious that his English friend Alaric Kent might. Kent is in Italy to study a little-known manuscript of Leonardo da Vinci which bears upon a play he is writing on the relationship of the painter and La Giaconda (Mona Lisa). Though Kent fights the growing impulse, he soon finds himself falling in love with Dione. After seeing her frequently, he comes to recognize in her character certain elements which enhance his understanding of the subject of Leonardo's most famous painting. Ultimately, Gigino gives him his blessing to court Dione; and, after plighting his troth with her before Pan's Mountain (he has said he cannot yet marry her in a traditional ceremony), they make love.

Not until she finds that she is pregnant does she learn that he is already married. Upon discovering this fact, she coaxes him to the top of the mountain, pushes him off a precipice, and tells Pan she is returning him. Years later she, Cecca, and her little boy are living in a small hut in the country. Dione is considered to be crazy by the peasants (she is still suffering from the shock, evidently); and she makes a living for the three of them by running a small dairy. The story ends with her singing one of her many Russian folk songs about a maiden whose lover has been drowned.

Like all the preceding works, this novel shows many strengths along with certain obvious weaknesses which should by now have been overcome. The main strength is an almost perfect parallel of character and setting. "I like to feel the earth under my toes," says Dione. "It likes to feel me, and I like to feel it"(6). The setting is of vast and mysterious beauty, and the natural child of this environment is both of these things. She is part of a "chain of being" which extends far back into the primeval past, and she has virtually no sense of time or of man-made place. There is a masterful tone in the story which suggests the primitive, the supernatural, the natural impulse.

It is unfortunate that this novel is weakened by two basic flaws. The first is the ending; but, reviewing the Princess' weaker stories, there seems to be a penchant for the inappropriate sensational ending. In *Pan's Mountain,* it evokes a feeling of sentimentality, which is certainly an emotion inferior to the objective unfolding of the love story. One can only assume that the Princess was more swayed by the emotion in the subject than by a rational appraisal of it, which is clearly not an indication of a mature artist. On the other hand, the characterization and the consistent tone of narration—always difficult to achieve—both indicate a high degree of control. Moreover, in terms of relative importance to the success of the story, the exaggerated ending is overshadowed by these considerations. One should regard such weaknesses, therefore, as interesting flaws in a generally well-executed novel.

The second major weakness—that of the chief male character—has a deeper significance. Perhaps the best method of approaching this problem is from character motivation. For approximately nine-tenths of the time that Alaric appears in the story, he is shown in a sympathetic light. He is brilliant and deferential to Dione; he seems a creature of conscience. Then, as if having been hidden behind a curtain throughout, a bad side is suddenly revealed—a side so full of deceit as to reverse all former opinion; and the reader feels that both he and Dione—perhaps also Alaric —have been played a dirty trick by the author for the sake of giving her heroine a chance to play her trump card.

Leaving the reader unprepared for the revelation of Alaric's deceit violates an unwritten law of literature which requires that an artist tell the whole truth about a character as the story progresses. The reasons behind this sudden reversal are significant, for Alaric Kent by no means stands by himself in this literary offense. Recalling Amélie's *According to St. John*, one is also reminded of a hero whose weak moral character induces his wife to commit sensational suicide. Then there is Trafford in *The Golden Rose* whose inability to sustain spiritual love gives Meraud the impetus to become a sort of martyr for love. In fact, taking Amélie's former male characters as a whole, the only two who stand out as strong personalities are Herod (in *Herod and Mariamne*) and Augustine (in *Augustine the Man*). And these were not powerful character creations so much as they were character adaptations from Josephus and St. Augustine's *Confessions*. There had been, in short, no strong male character creations. Jock Dering in *Barbara Dering* (though not in *The Quick or the Dead?*) had come close, but one sees the admirable qualities of his character in fits and starts. Considering the entire canon, there are only three males who are portrayed as possessing any notable depth; and all three were created after *Pan's Mountain*.

Several reasons might be advanced to explain the presence of this succession of weak males who contrast with the strong, dashing heroines. The first is the author's towering ego—a force which caused her to project herself in her fiction. Second, perhaps, are her ideas of feminism, which were closely allied to this ego. In 1914, when she was interviewed by the New York *Times* on the subject of feminism, at the time a popular national issue, she indicated that her interest in the subject was far from political. She was, significantly, interested in it for reasons which affect the ego. "As for the vote, that does not so much matter," she said. "It is relatively unimportant for women to have the right of suffrage. It is the inner life that matters; the point of view. . . ." [6] In other words, women as personalities were to have the same place as men.

In the same interview, Amélie stated that in marriage, there should be "sex cooperation," or an equally important position for women as for men. She also stated a belief in "complete comraderie," which meant that husband and wife should be friends as well as marriage partners. These were extremely sophisticated notions for the times, when patriarchy still held sway for the most part. Though such avant-garde ideas are not especially surprising for the Princess, it is unusual, in light of her fiction, that she should speak for a system which implied male equality. It may well be, then, that she unconsciously reduced her male characters to a position inferior to that of her females. In any event, the shallow depiction of male characters was to change as she approached her period of highest achievement.

IV   Hidden House (1912)

Princess Troubetzkoy showed considerable interest in supernatural phenomena throughout her life. Numerous oral accounts exist which tell of séances held at Castle Hill, and at least one reliable written source relates her sincere belief in a ghost who made frequent appearances at the house.[7] In *The Golden Rose,* she had ingenuously spoken of Meraud Cabell's ability to project her mind to far removed places as if doing so were a common human characteristic. It is little wonder, then, that Amélie should have written two ghost novels.

The supernatural topic of *Hidden House,* the first of these, is metempsychosis, or the transmigration of souls. According to Plato, the souls of the dead abide in the bodies of animals and other men until their eventual integration into the godhead. The Princess saw fictional potential in the Platonic theory by speculating on the possibility that two souls might alternately occupy the same body.

In the beginning of the story, the reader is told that Moina and Robina Jardine are both granddaughters of the aged master of a large manse hidden in the mountains of Virginia. Marston, the young New Englander from whose point of view the story is related, at first believes that the two girls are separate entities. Shortly after arriving at Hidden House, he meets Moina, with whom he soon falls in love. When he tells his feelings to Mr. Jardine, the old man suggests that, before committing himself, he wait until he has seen the second granddaughter, Robina, who is soon coming to care for him.

Her appearance a few days later is both unexpected and mysterious. Marston first sees her singing and dancing up the road which runs past the family cemetery. He watches, overwhelmed, as she bounds over the iron cemetery fence and begins dancing on a grave marked by a stone containing the name Robina Jardine, but no dates. This latter fact is significant, as she appears to be a creature of no particular time or place; moreover, old Jardine has cryptically stated that there has always been a Robina in the family and that he hopes there always will be.

Robina writes poems about ghosts; she refers to God as "an old man outworn by the ages";[8] she tells Marston that all of iife—he and God included—are mad. He nevertheless falls in love with her; and, just after their one and only kiss, she warns him that anyone who kisses her lips will "go sweetly mad" (112). Whereupon she exclaims that a voice is calling her in the distance and that it is speaking Moina's name. Half entranced, she screams for a servant, who comes and takes her home. After she has been put to bed, the old man explains that she has had another of the seizures to which she is susceptible but which can be prevented if Marston marries her. But, when Marston sees her a few hours later, he looks into the eyes not of Robina but of Moina. He calls her by the latter's name, but she insists that she is really Robina. Whether from shock over the change of identity, or in fulfillment of the curse for having kissed Robina, Marston falls into a delirium which debilitates him mentally and physically for several weeks.

During his recuperation, he is told that Robina is actually a spirit which frequently attacks the soul of a young female member of the family in an attempt to dislodge it from its natural body and take its place. Unless the body of the victim is killed, the spirit will establish herself there. Though Marston tries his best to determine whether Moina and Robina are really two different girls, or simply two souls alternately occupying the same body, he is never certain. With his pondering, the story ends, as have so many well-known stories of its genre. For example, did Hawthorne's Goodman Brown really see the witches or not? Were Henry James's Peter Quince and Miss Jessel of *The Turn of the Screw* really visible or not? Did Poe's Ligeia really appear in the

body of the Lady Rowena or not? The possible amount of speculation is infinite.

Amélie's story is extremely well written, and the reader is at first
introduced into a world of reality with which he can easily identify. Then, when he finds that the borders of this world merge
with the supernatural, the author brings the reader's sense of reality into frightful focus. The story is unusual among the Princess'
fiction in featuring a male protagonist who is neither a stereo-
typed hero nor a villain but a touchstone of reality by whom the
reader can gauge the strange events. Moreover, Marston is also
the first-person narrator; so the reader can sense firsthand his reactions. The story bears traces of the old trademark of the overpowering female in the person of Robina, who is quick to tell Marston
that he needs to drink more deeply from the cup of vitality.
Nevertheless, the author intends the reader's sympathy to be with
Marston, as hers clearly is.

V   *1914*

If one could select an all-round good year from the life of Princess Troubetzkoy, it would surely be 1914. In July of the preceding year, she had finished the manuscript of *World's-End,* the best
book she would ever write; and, by the beginning of the new year,
five installments had appeared in *Collier's.* In February, her own
fortunes prosperous, she played in a movie called *The Case of the
Poor Author,* in which she performed some of the opening scenes
from *The Quick or the Dead?* [9] In late April, she and the Prince
sailed for England, where they were the guests of George Curzon
at Hackwood, his country estate. In June, they were guests of
honor at a dinner given by the prime minister Lord Oxford and
his wife, the former Margot Asquith, a member of the "Souls."
That same month novelist George Moore asked to see the manuscript of *Shadows of Flames,* her next novel. In mid-July the
Troubetzkoys set out for the Lago Maggiore, where a member of
the family reported their brilliant season in London—that the
Prince had received many portrait orders and that there was great
prosperity in general. [10]

During this busy year all was well with her career and with the
country she dearly loved. Yet, even in that pleasant summer, tragedy was slowly approaching. For, as she later related to Emily

Clark, she had sailed for England at an inconvenient moment because she sensed that the England she knew was no longer a permanent institution.[11] While she was Lord Curzon's guest, Archduke Francis Ferdinand was assassinated in Sarajevo; and she
was never to see either Lord Curzon or England again.

VI   World's-End (1913–14)

World's-End proved to be one of those rare combinations in the
world of letters in which a solid artistic achievement is given de-
servedly high praise in the form of criticism and large sales. After
it finished its run in *Collier's* in April, 1914, it was issued as a
book;[12] and by July 15, when the Troubetzkoys left England for
the Lago Maggiore, it was already in its fourth English printing.
It was to sell upward of a hundred thousand copies in England
alone, not to mention many more thousands in the United States.

Once more, it is primarily the story of a young woman of feeling and intellect; but this time—for the first time—she is matched
with a man of equally admirable qualities. The man, Owen Randolph, has, at forty-seven, never married; and he has little pros-
pect of ever doing so. One of the main reasons is that he is the self-
appointed guardian of his nephew Richard Bryce and to only a
slightly lesser degree of his sister Sally, Richard's mother. Sally's
husband had died several years before without having rebuilt the
fortune he had lost, and the wealthy Owen is supporting both
Sally and Richard as members of New York high society.

One wonders how anyone could be so magnanimous, for Richard is a perfect fop. He is first seen just after a sojourn in France,
where he has supposedly been studying art. Yet he is much more a
gay social blade than an artist, and he goes about proclaiming
that religion and marriage are institutions beneath his advanced
sense of values. Though Owen shudders when he thinks that
Richard will some day inherit World's-End, his Virginia plantation, he dismisses his libertine ideas as a sowing of intellectual
wild oats. Moreover, Sally is little more attractive than her
offspring. A virtual parasite to Owen, she repays his generosity
with selfishness and ingratitude. A few years before the story
commences, she has considered instituting lunacy proceedings
against her brother for having sold stock in oil companies with
unfair labor practices. She thought him demented for using his

profits to buy cotton mills which cut working hours to eight per day, would not tolerate child labor, and offered profit-sharing.

Owen has just returned from a trip to Georgia, where he has studied a number of private schools with a view to establishing similar ones for his workers. His major fear in leaving World's-End to Richard is that Richard may be unkind to these people. He discusses his misgivings in New York with his cousin Mary Talliaferro (pronounced "Tolliver"), who sympathizes with his views of Richard, but for a different reason: on one occasion she has seen him powder his nose before going on a ride with a young lady. Though having many good reasons for disliking Richard, Owen and Mary resolve to try to change him by inviting Phoebe Nelson, their young cousin, to World's-End for a stay in the summer. They think that Phoebe, an extremely level-headed young woman, may prove a healthful influence.

Owen soon returns to World's-End, and it is not long before he meets Phoebe. She is pictured as being more Victorian than modern, which means that she is somewhat romantic; indeed, she dreams of a prince charming who will come and take her away as a bride. She dares to dream that it might be Owen, but she realizes that he is an improbable fulfillment of her dream since he is so much older than she. Nevertheless, a rapport is established between them. However, when Richard arrives, Phoebe recognizes him as the hero she has romanticized. He, ever the effete artist, sees her in purely artistic terms. Apparently, love has never stirred in his heart, and to him she is a promising subject for a portrait and nothing more. She has a pet crow named "Jimmy Toots" (one notes once again the heroine's attraction for birds), and he proposes to do a portrait of her and this pet which he will call "Pandore et le Génie du Coffre." As he paints, he feels strange stirrings within, and suddenly he realizes that "any other man" would have loved Phoebe long before. Still, he continues to paint without falling, or so he considers it, to the level of other men. Finally he kisses her, which makes her feel that love has finally arrived. The next day Richard returns, but this time he gets stranded by a thunderstorm at Nelson's Gift, the family home in which Phoebe lives with her aging father. That night, when Richard, unable to sleep, goes into the garden, he is soon followed by Phoebe. In a little Greek temple in the garden, he surrenders to his passion and makes love to her.

She innocently believes his love to be sincere, even though he has already told her that he thinks marriage a social convention that is followed merely to please the world. Since she is hopeful that he will become her husband in the conventional way, she is startled when she receives word the next day that "business" has suddenly called him to New York. He includes no address there, but even this fact does not mar her ideal of him. However, as time goes on, she becomes more and more agitated, both because she has expected something quite different from real love and because she begins to receive paraphrased French poems from him which, posing as letters, neither begin with a proper salutation nor end with an expression of love. When she discovers that she is pregnant, this knowledge creates such an emotional state that, when Owen returns from New York, he senses her problem intuitively. By this time, she has told Richard; and he answers, in effect, that he is willing to send her money enough to go to a secluded farm in New England, where she can have the child and where he can continue to be her lover. This offer, of course, shocks her, as does the news that he has slipped away on an Oriental trip with a boorish male friend. This news even shocks the shrewish Sally who, in her impersonal way, says she will help Phoebe.

It is Owen, however, who takes the first positive action. He decides to ask Mary to stay with Phoebe; but, on his way to get her, instinct tells him to go to Nelson's Gift. He arrives just in time to see Phoebe running through the forest with a bottle of chloroform. Not only does he save her from suicide but, spurred by a combination of compassion and love for her and a real hatred for Richard, he asks her to marry him. Though she has always dreamed of Owen as her prince charming, she is confused and distraught by the recent sequence of events. Nevertheless, she accepts his proposal, more out of not knowing what to do than from real love. They are married the following Monday, and they leave immediately for Europe. They spend some time in France and even more in England with a group of intellectual politicians obviously modeled after the "Souls." As Princess Troubetzkoy had done, Phoebe becomes the star of the group, and all think her witty and beautiful. While there, her pregnancy becomes known to all. And here, several months later, her baby—Susan Diana—is born.

The marriage has naturally left Sally disconsolate, for she realizes that Richard will now be deprived of his inheritance. He, of

course, knows nothing about it and hears nothing at all until he is
on his way home. Owen, in the meantime, knows that the baby is
Richard's, but Phoebe has said nothing of this to him. She fears,
quite naturally, that, if she does, he will no longer love her. Neither can he say anything to her, also quite naturally, as this would
call her integrity into question. She comes very close to telling him
on two occasions, but she loses heart. He tries in every way he
knows to get her to tell him the truth, as her knowledge is obviously a great psychological burden to her. He even goes as far as
to introduce such topics as Guinevere's infidelity and Arthur's forgiveness, but to no avail.

By this time, Richard has returned and, for the sake of appearances, visits World's-End. Phoebe treats him with cool civility;
but, on one occasion, when she sees him while out walking, she is
so agitated that she drops her gloves in fright. He picks them up
for her, and she silently turns and walks away. When she has gone
a few yards, she drops them again, as if they were dirty. At
Christmas, when he returns for another visit, he brings gifts for
all; and she burns the Chinese silk robe with gold buttons that he
has brought her. Richard's towering ego will not permit such
treatment, and the tension grows. His desire is now to humiliate
her, and he gets his chance one day when they meet on a path. He
will not let her pass, and he begins telling her that he thinks her
behavior toward him is ridiculous. Just as he mentions that she
has been his mistress, Owen walks up, strikes him with the stick
he is carrying, and then proceeds to beat him to within an inch of
his life. As a matter of fact, it is feared for a long time that Richard will die. When he finally recovers and leaves with his mother,
Sally has softened somewhat and is even partially forgiving; and
Owen has remembered Richard handsomely in his will. After the
beating, Phoebe has told the forgiving Owen the truth about her
and Richard; and the novel ends with Phoebe pregnant with what
she hopes will be Owen's own heir.

Reviews of *World's-End* were consistently laudatory. Phoebe
Nelson headed the list of its notable qualities, and the reviewer
for *Review of Reviews* summarized the sentiments of his fellows
when he proclaimed, "The novelist has never drawn a character
more human and appealing than that of Phoebe Nelson, the
simple Virginia girl." [13]

As for Owen, a New York *Times* commentator stated that, if it be possible for a man to be as good as Owen, "it is surely well that our jealous conventions should be given a jolt, and a new idea given us of generosity in marriage." [14]

That the two principals should have been appealing to reviewers, especially to tough-minded ones like the New York *Times* man, is significant. This fact is but one detail in the picture of achievement, however, and should be seen in the light of more important qualities for proper illumination. Attractive though Phoebe may be, her major importance is that she exists on an emotional level more familiar to readers than that occupied by any of her predecessors. Where former heroines had a perfection of character and a power of emotion which were virtually superhuman, Phoebe shows a susceptibility to temptation and a vexation under guilt which are common to mankind in general. Thus, she is more completely Realistic than any earlier Rives protagonist.

Another significant distinction is the growth Phoebe undergoes in the course of the novel. This expansion mirrors both the development of her creator and that of the literary age in which she was currently writing. Phoebe begins as a girl in her late teens who, like so many young women of the Victorian era, has romantic fantasies of what love should be—fantasies which the Princess time and time again projected in the fiction of her early period. When these dreams led to no more success in Phoebe's life than they did in the Princess' career, Phoebe, like Amélie, is forced to face the stern realities of her folly; but she does so without ever compromising her enthusiasm for living or her strength of character. In the case of the Princess, divorce and economic vicissitudes had made her more realistic without making her lose her profound *joie de vivre*. The character of Phoebe, like that of the Princess, is composed of a broad spectrum of emotions and of a depth which contains much worldly wisdom.

The advance in Realism represented by Phoebe might be sufficient reason in itself for calling *World's-End* superior to Amélie's former novels. It should be noted, however, that, while growth in the depiction of heroines can be construed as significant artistic progress, it is, after all, progress within a limited sphere. This development has been traced in foregoing pages, but often accompanied by disparaging comments about other aspects of the works which feature outstanding heroines. More often than not, these comments have been aimed at male characters and at arbitrary plot manipulations. *World's-End* makes a successful break from this mold, for the scope of its Realism is wider than that of any novel Amélie ever wrote. Supporting characters have a life of their own, and they are not placed in the story simply for support of the heroine. As a matter of fact, when seen in terms of the other characters, Phoebe is at times rather weak and powerless. She possesses throughout strong character fiber, but she is certainly not placed on a white charger and made a challenge to the others.

Owen is the best example of a character type who has come into his own in this novel. A multifaceted gentleman, he is seen as humane, generous, indulgent, gentle, well-bred; but, when the occasion demands, he is hard, even violent. He is, bar none, the most completely developed and most appealing of Amélie's male characters. In addition, Richard is more than the conventional cad. He is spoiled and deceitful; there is a strong hint that he is effeminate; but in the end he is shown tempered by the punishment for his evildoing.

The powerful conflict of these characters, each vivid in his own right, makes *World's-End* the author's masterpiece. Former efforts leave the reader at best sympathetic to the heroine or, as with *Barbara Dering*, with a glimmer of hope for the future. More often, however, one is left with a certain revulsion over a maudlin tragedy brought in at the last minute, as in *According to St. John* and in *Witness of the Sun*. But with *World's End* one is left with a feeling that approaches Aristotelian catharsis. Throughout the lengthy narrative, one suffers with the frustrating position of Phoebe and at the caddish Richard's unavenged iniquities. In the end this frustration is relieved, but through no magical machinations. Richard is made to pay; and Phoebe is finally able to tell Owen of her indiscretion. Yet all have received wounds that will never completely heal. There are no innocent promises of a carefree future—only the hope offered by forgiveness and the potential of life to renew itself.

Willa Cather had accused Amélie Rives of having been "entirely unnatural" in an earlier book. "There is no remedy for that," she had said. "If one does not see at least a few things as they are by the time one is twenty, then one never sees them at all and goes through life with distorted vision. . . ." [15] One can only guess what Miss Cather would have thought of *World's-End* and of her early prophecy. In any event, if *World's-End* does not contain a view of "things as they are," then one is not likely ever to see them in Amélie's fiction.

VII   Shadows of Flames (*1914–15*)

On June 15, 1914, Princess Troubetzkoy wrote her sister Landon Rives from London[16] that George Moore had asked to read the manuscript of *Shadows of Flames,* her next novel. Just what the author of *Esther Waters* thought of the work is not recorded, but one may speculate that he was impressed. The author was riding a wave of success from *World's-End,* and the new book compared favorably with it. Exactly one month later, the Princess accepted a check of five thousand dollars from *Cosmopolitan* for the serial rights.

The novel is the story of the three loves of Sophy Taliaferro Chesney. Her first is Cecil Chesney, a young British nobleman. During their three-year marriage, they have actively participated in London society. Of late, he is alternately extremely depressed and moody, then unnaturally elated. It is soon discovered that he is addicted to dope. In the first scene, he refuses to go to a party with his wife; he prefers to stay home to peruse a book of filthy prints. In these moods, he is often abusive to Sophy. The situation is made worse for Sophy because Lady Wychcote, her mother-in-law, hates her and all other Americans; and she believes that Sophy has driven Cecil to dope addiction. At the party which Cecil has refused to attend, Sophy meets the Marchese Marco Amaldi, a friend of the lover of her friend Olive Arundel. He obviously falls in love with Sophy immediately; and, though she feels drawn to him, she never thinks of having an affair. In fact, she deplores Olive's doing so. Nevertheless, a rapport is established, and they become friends.

If not an actual re-enactment, this scene is clearly reminiscent of the meeting of the Troubetzkoys. Both Amaldi and the Prince were from the Lago Maggiore region; both had American mothers; both realized immediately that they had found the one love of their lives. Moreover, the group among whom they met is the same; for there are scenes which are clearly a continuation of those in *World's-End* which recall the "Souls." Sophy is very much like the Princess: she is from an old Virginia plantation (Sweet-

Waters) and has published a book, *The Shadow of A Flame*, in
her youth which has made her famous; and finally, a character
whom Sophy and Amaldi meet at a later gathering is clearly modeled after Oscar Wilde. Called Oswald Tyne in the story, he
greets Sophy by saying, "Thank you for being so pale tonight,
dear lady. . . . One gets so weary of colour at times. . . ."[17]

Sophy has attended this function with Chesney, who embar-
rasses her by suddenly calling to her at the top of his voice, for no
reason whatever, "You lie!" Though the conversation stops at this
outburst, everyone deftly turns to other topics; and he leaves by
himself. The next morning, the butler tells her that Chesney is in a
kind of coma. Sophy soon discovers that he is addicted to both
morphine and cocaine. Though treatments are begun immediately, he is able, by wily artifices, to continue the habit for some
weeks undetected. This burdensome pattern soon endangers
Sophy's health, and she is advised by the family doctor to take a
holiday away from Chesney. She and her son, Bobby, go to Italy
where she soon meets Amaldi by accident. She meets his mother
shortly thereafter, and for a time the three enjoy an innocent companionship.

When Chesney, improved and stronger, arrives in Italy, he and
Amaldi become casual friends. They sail together, and on one of
their outings Chesney contracts sciatica. When his pain grows intense, he resorts to dope. Though he eventually recovers from the
sciatica attack and is able to withdraw once more from narcotics,
he is accidentally drowned in the Lago Maggiore just as he is
preparing to return to England with Sophy and Bobby. Sophy,
heartbroken over Chesney's death and feeling partially responsible
for Bobby's delicate health, decides to return with her son to
Sweet-Waters (here again, a place of calm security).

Here her third love begins—with Morris Loring, who is quite
obviously modeled after Chanler. Loring first meets Sophy when
he comes to Sweet-Waters to visit her sister Charlotte and her
husband, Judge Joe Macon. Loring is much younger than Sophy,
and is very handsome. Though he falls in love with her, she will
not encourage his suit, feeling that love has passed for her. He
persists, however; and she eventually accepts him. Loring, like
Chanler, is unbelievably wealthy and also somewhat spoiled and
used to having his own way. Nevertheless, the two are quite
happy for a time. They live both in New York and Newport. He

calls her Seléné, and he is proud to play Endymion; but the luster
of their marriage gradually begins to dim. One of the main reasons for the change is bad blood between him and Bobby, who
does not like his new foster father. Also, there are times when
Loring equates Bobby with Chesney.

Always a hard drinker, Loring gradually moves in the direction
of alcoholism. As he does so, his relationship with Sophy begins to
deteriorate. He becomes so jealous of her that he resents her returning to Sweet-Waters for a visit. She goes anyway; and, when
she returns to New York, he tempers his drinking somewhat. The
situation improves when the two go to England. Here they live
happily until Loring insults an aged statesman, is gently scolded
for doing so, and thence returns to America. The final rift now
begins. Belinda Horton, stepdaughter of Loring's aunt, is about
to make her debut at Newport. Ever since Loring has kissed her
in a fit of passion two years before while a bachelor, she has been
madly in love with him. Sophy invites the girl to stay with her and
Loring; and, while there, Belinda tempts Loring until he suc-
cumbs.

In the meantime, Amaldi has arrived in the United States to
lecture at Columbia University, and he senses the adultery of Belinda and Loring long before Sophy does. When she finally discovers it, she returns to Sweet-Waters, after telling Loring that
she intends to leave him. At first, he tries to turn the tables on her,
saying that she and Amaldi are lovers; but then, worn down by
alcohol and by the shock of what she tells him, he collapses with a
kind of nervous prostration. She eventually goes to South Dakota
(as the Princess had done), where she is granted a divorce in six
months.

During this period, she has been soothed with letters from
Amaldi; but she is uprooted suddenly by the news of the death of
Gerald Chesney, Cecil's brother. She goes to England immediately, to find that she has been handsomely provided for in Gerald's will. For one thing, she has inherited Breene, a fine, but
small Tudor country house, and she goes there to live with Bobby,
now Lord Wychcote. Amaldi, living in London, where his music is
enjoying high favor, visits her often. When Lady Wychcote warns
her of the possibility of a scandal, Sophy accepts the warning
fairly calmly. However, when Amaldi declares his love for her,
they decide that it will be better to separate temporarily. No

sooner have they done so than Sophy hears that a Count Amaldi has been in an accident. It turns out to have been the brother of her Count Amaldi, but Lady Wychcote's brother Colonel Bolling-ham has seen her going into the Amaldi house just after the acci-dent and has concluded that her visit was an assignation.

One of the main reasons Amaldi and Sophy have never dis-cussed marriage is that Amaldi has been married in Italy, where there is no divorce. Even though his wife is a promiscuous adul-teress and he has not lived with her for many years, no way exists to break the marital contract. If, however, he changes citizenship, he could obtain a divorce; so he now plans to become a Swiss citizen. Though Sophy thinks his doing so a great sacrifice, she does not discourage him. After he has visited in Italy a while, he sends for her to come for a visit with him and his mother in Venice. Shortly after she arrives, Lady Wychcote suddenly appears. Though the two women seem to get on fairly well, one evening while Sophy is visiting Amaldi's mother, the marchesa has a fall; and Sophy, who stays on to look after her, does not get home until early morning. Lady Wychcote is waiting for her; but, though she seems rather distant, she only tells Sophy that she is going to take Bobby to Murano for the day. Instead of doing so, she takes him to England. When Sophy finally arrives to retrieve her son, she finds the boy delirious with pneumonia: he had stolen out of the house the night before in an attempt to get to the railroad station and thence to her. He has sensed Lady Wychcote's attempt to keep him in custody (she has thought she had sufficient evidence to prove Sophy an unfit guardian).

Bobby recovers, but Sophy has decided that she will not com-promise him by falling in love again. However, the story ends with her thinking of the swifts she has seen in Venice; and these birds, symbolic of her recent Italian experience, are of course symbolic of Amaldi also. As she remembers them, they seem to soar in her mind high above the English rooks outside her window. One is left with the hope that perhaps love will conquer in the end.

Following closely upon *World's-End, Shadows of Flames* con-tains many strengths found in the earlier book. Once again, the Realism is of broad scope and is manifest especially in supporting characters. Chesney is drawn with particular brilliance. His is the deteriorating mind of the addict, with its sudden shifts, its illogic,

its fantasies. Charlotte and Joe Macon, two anachronistic southern-
ers of the Victorian era, are also drawn with the sure touch of the
master artist; but Loring, a weak and impetuous overgrown boy,
is the most vivid creation of all.

The novel fails to measure up to its predecessor, however, primarily because it is not plotted so effectively. Where *World's-End*
had moved unswervingly toward an ultimate climax, *Shadows of
Flames* is somewhat repetitious. The males involved in Sophy's
three love affairs differ markedly as individuals, but all three epi-
sodes result in essentially the same frustration for her. Moreover,
she is essentially the same person at the beginning of the story as
at the end; and her display of forbearance after each of her romantic misadventures shows little, if any, variation.

Interest is maintained in Phoebe Nelson because she is shown
as unfolding and as progressing to new plateaus of activity and
understanding. By contrast, Sophy is rather too static. In addition,
her character is none too brilliantly defined in the first place.
Granted, Phoebe Nelson was a difficult act to follow; but Sophy
does not come close to her in vividness. She is courageous, long-
suffering, generous, honest, and strong willed enough to challenge
social convention; but these qualities do not cohere to form a distinctive entity. Virtues by themselves are insufficient to give the
indefinable *je ne sais quoi* which characterizes unique fictional
personages.

Of course, Phoebe Nelson's adventures had not been experienced by the author. This protagonist could therefore be viewed
from some distance and with an objective eye. But the unhappily
married Sophy had sprung from an intimate corner of her
creator's memory, and it is far more difficult to express such a
character in terms which a reader can visualize. A character may
be forceful without being vivid, however, and all of Sophy's struggles are powerful conflicts. The somber result is her satisfaction in
having acted all along in good conscience even though her actions
were misconstrued by her enemies. Expectations of future happiness with Amaldi are as elusive as the remembered songs of the
Italian swifts.

The apparent theme is stoical endurance, which does not neces-
sarily lead to tangible rewards but which ennobles the spirit in
practice. One infers this theme from Sophy's explanation of the

title of her early volume of poems, *The Shadow of A Flame:* "I had stayed awake all night—reading by candle-light. My window looked to the east. When the sun rose, my candle was still burning. And as I started to blow it out, I noticed that in the sunlight, its flame cast a shadow on the page of my book. And it came to me that we were all like that—like little flames casting shadows in some greater light. And that our passions were also like little flames that cast their shadows—of sorrow . . . regret . . . despair . . . weariness . . . ." (227). Sophy's unhappy marriages are but shadows of love. It is as if she were one of the people, seated on the floor of the cave in Plato's *Republic*, who see the world only as a reflection in a mirror illuminated by a fire. In short, her final situation is tragic in that she is forced to exist in the world of shadow and never in the realm of pure flame.

The idea of flame plays an important role as well. It is the main motif of a well-developed system of imagery and symbolism which acts as a cohesive factor in the novel. Examples of flame imagery are seen in the description of Sophy's feelings between her marriages. Chesney's love is described as in ashes, and she is pictured as a phoenix when she feels the new flame of Loring's love (314). When the second marriage begins to weaken, Loring is pictured as burning in an evil flame of passion (429). When Sophy goes to Venice, she realizes that she is really giving Amaldi the shadow of a flame for love—not the actual emotion itself but its reflection. But she also realizes that "This shadow was, after all, cast by a flame . . . ." (541).

A review in the New York *Times* is representative of critical opinion in saying that "The story as a whole is full of color, with a certain exuberance and passion which are rather unusual; clean, hotblooded, yet tempestuous, yet restrained; frank, but never offensive. . . . An interesting, well written, and carefully thought out book is *Shadows of Flames*." [18] An artist of the Princess' interests and abilities might hope to write many *Damsel Errants*, which she did; a few *Shadows of Flames*; but only one *World's-End*. After *World's-End*, one could expect little but anticlimax. The value of *Shadows of Flames* is that it has fallen so slightly from the acme.

VIII   *The War Years and the Stage*

The coming of World War I and all that it meant in terms of a changed Europe prevented the Troubetzkoys from ever again crossing the Atlantic. They could not bear to think of changes in a way of life which they had known to be grand and elegant. They now lived at Castle Hill during the warm months of the year and in New York during the winter. Here, despite the war, the Prince could paint, and the Princess could pursue her literary career. Her interests now turned more and more to the theater, and she began in 1916 a series of rather popular plays on the Broadway stage with *The Fear Market*. Though never published, this play ran at the Booth Theatre for a hundred and eighteen nights. A comedy, it concerns a retired colonel who operates a scandal magazine and blackmails his victims. One of the figures attacked is a young man who falls in love with the colonel's daughter, who, not knowing of her father's participation, decides to expose the blackmail ring. When she has to choose between her father and her lover, love triumphs. Though the piece was considered to be generally entertaining, reviewers found many faults with it. It was called melodramatic; its plot was said to be weak; the ending could be seen from the first. Nevertheless, in 1919, the Princess received a first installment of forty-five hundred dollars for the motion picture rights. The picture, which appeared in 1920, starred Alice Brady in the role of the colonel's daughter.

The stage success of *The Fear Market* was followed in August, 1918, by *Allegiance*. Had this play been published, it would doubtlessly hold more interest for modern readers than *The Fear Market*, as an anti-German play and a piece of propaganda literature. Though the New York *Times* reviewer did not think the drama developed until the last of the three acts, he pointed out the favorable audience reaction to the anti-German raillery in the first act.[19] The play concerns a father's change of heart toward Kaiser Wilhelm whom he supports early in the play, and the change is caused by his father's being struck with apoplexy on learning of the sinking of the *Lusitania* and by his son's being blinded by a Prussian oculist. However, the play also cries out for sympathy for German immigrants not loyal to the kaiser. It is frequently stated that Prince Troubetzkoy was co-author of this and several other of the Princess' dramas, but unfortunately there is no way of being certain just how much he contributed to the collaboration. All the same, it is easy to see how he could have figured strongly in a play about immigrants to America which spoke for tolerance of these foreign nationals.

IX   The Ghost Garden (*1918*)

Allegiance was followed in 1918 by *The Ghost Garden*, Princess Troubetzkoy's second attempt at a ghost story. It featured, as had *Hidden House*, a New Englander (Evan Radford), who arrives in Virginia for a holiday. His host is called away, and he is left in the care of a Mr. Warrenger and his daughter Melany. They live at Hilton, a Virginia plantation close to Her Wish, another large estate, whose main house is supposed to be haunted. Before Radford visits Hilton, he and Joel Carver, a local farmer, visit Her Wish; and Radford has the feeling that he has been there before and even wanders through the Euonymous maze with no problem at all. Then he and Carver hear the sound of spinning.

When Radford arrives at Hilton, Mr. Warrenger relates the story of Her Wish, which was built by a Colonel Horsemanden for his daughter Melany as one of her many wishes. She was a strong-willed girl who would not marry the one man she loved because he refused to change his surname to hers and to give up all his other property and live at Her Wish. A creature of the strongest will, she died unmarried; and her spirit is still supposedly present in the house.

Radford is interested in the possibility of ghosts—or, more specifically, in the people who believe in them. He is therefore struck with the unusual Melany Warrenger, a descendant of the Horsemandens, who has had a beautiful voice which she has lost and which she believes the jealous ghost of the first Melany has taken from her. Preoccupied and withdrawn, she is quite afraid of the ghost and the thrall in which she believes it holds her. Radford quite expectedly falls in love with Melany and vows to protect her by matching his will against the ghost's. He believes if he spends a night in the house, he will exorcise the spirit.

Radford is in no way superstitious; but, as mentioned above, he is intellectually interested in ghosts and in those who believe in them. During the night he spends at Her Wish, he falls asleep while reading *Mandeville's Travels;* and he awakens to feel a coldness about him (a common sign of ghosts). When the first Melany's clock, which has apparently not run for years, begins to run, a carved skeleton on top of the clock turns toward him, then disappears, and in its place a damask rose appears. He takes the rose to be a "message of capitulation," believing that he has conquered the ghost's will. When he convinces Melany that he has done so, they begin to make marriage plans. He is rather cocksure —so much so that he allows Mr. Warrenger to give Her Wish to him and Melany as a wedding present, despite Melany's misgivings.

He has come to believe the line that the Princess would one day have carved on her husband's tombstone, "Love is strong as death." But, when he moves into Her Wish with his servants, he begins to see that the rose, instead of indicating capitulation, was actually a harbinger of the ghost's return. No sooner does he note its scent than the ghost appears. Tension mounts as the wedding day approaches and as the ghost continues to appear. In the early morning hours of the anticipated day the specter appears more vivid than ever, and, dressed as a bride, leads Radford through the house and out into the rose garden to the grave of Melany Horsemanden. Radford is by now obsessed with holding on to his own spirit and not resigning it to the apparition; but, when the creature turns to him, bares its face, and stares into his eyes, he loses control of his will and swoons.

In the meantime, Melany, who has dreamed the incident, gets up and starts running for Her Wish. When she arrives, she finds Radford prostrate on the grave. She now sees the situation as a challenge to her own will, for she never believes for a moment that he is dead. She sees the situation as a kind of Manichaean duality: she is the power of light; the jealous spirit, the power of darkness. The local physician, Doctor Borridge, believes Radford dead; but Melany believes him entranced and will not leave his side. Finally, three days later, she calls his name; and he rouses, though he is left with a sense of weightiness and for a time does not perceive her. But he gradually recovers, resumes his marriage plans, and finally tells his experiences to a psychiatric doctor who warns him against returning to Her Wish. Though his need to go becomes obsessive, he is restrained, falls asleep, and awakens with

a stronger urge than ever to return. Again he is restrained, but this
time he falls into a trance. When he awakens, he tells Melany that
he has "won," that his love has been stronger than the ghost, and
that the ghost has finally gone forever. He does not realize that
during his sleep Her Wish has burned to the ground from a fire,
which, it is suggested, his bride has set. Though he has saved his
spirit, he is ever thereafter subject to a "strange emotion" every
time he smells roses or sees the iridescence of cobwebs or of ocean
foam.

Reviewers called *The Ghost Garden* a new kind of ghost story,
one in which the central mystery was enhanced by the attractive
setting, the love interest, and the beauty of the ghost. While it is
true that these elements create a more attractive milieu than do
the austere Gothic accoutrements of many mystery stories (Poe's
Tales of the Grotesque and Arabesque, for instance), they also
have the negative effect of diluting the central conflict of mystery.
Initially, the conflict concerns finding out the truth behind the
strange events taking place at Her Wish—a good, legitimate premise for a mystery plot. Then Radford falls in love, which can also
be a legitimate incident in a good mystery story; however, this
element is elevated to the level of the initial conflict by becoming
inextricably entwined with it. No longer can the ghost be seen as a
supernatural phenomenon; it becomes an insidious force threatening to destroy the budding romance with which the reader has
come to sympathize. The tendency, therefore, is to concentrate on
the romance of Radford and Melany and to disdain the ghost,
which is a rather ridiculous thing to do, since this apparition was
the center of interest in the beginning.

Quite simply, one reads mystery stories for the sake of the mystery; and other elements are subordinate to it. *The Turn of the
Screw*, for instance, has negligible romantic or other elements besides the central mystery, yet it has been read for generations as a
powerful tale of suspense. *The Ghost Garden* is not read today;
and, while it may be overstating the case to say that its divided
purpose is the cause of its lack of popularity, it is surely a factor.

It seems likely that the author was either uncertain of the ultimate direction of her plot when she began, or that she lost control
somewhere along the way. For it is obvious that she did not realize that simply as a suspense story *The Ghost Garden* is quite

effective. Actually advertised as a "suspense story" in the same
year of its publication by English publishers Hurst and Blackett, it
was published under the title *The Elusive Lady*.

X   The Prince and the Pauper (*1919*)

The Princess' long run of successful dramas was followed in
1919 by still another successful play, an adaptation of Samuel
Clemens's *The Prince and the Pauper*, which appeared at the
Booth Theatre early in November. The *Times* critic generally
praised the production, saying, "The old story is told with a good
deal of charm. . . ." [20] It should be noted, however, that the play
was not adapted from the book itself, but from an 1889 adaptation by Abby Sage Richardson, literary assistant to Daniel Froh-
man, who had first produced the play in Philadelphia during the
Christmas season of that year. The Princess "generally renovated"
the Richardson version by expanding, for instance, the subordinate role of Miles Hendon; for she knew that the part would
be taken by the well-known actor William Faversham. Other
changes included more focusing upon the prince in the guise of
the pauper than in the original story in order to avoid frequent
changes of scene. Tom Canty, the pauper boy, is emphasized only
in acts one and four.

It is not known just why the Princess turned to this popular
story at this time in her life. There was, of course, the abiding
interest in Clemens there had always been; but it seems that it
might have been more appropriate for her to have adapted the
story earlier, as she was often in New York during the last decade
of Clemens's life, and letters exist which show that there was mu-
tual admiration between them and that they dined together.
Whatever the reason, the adaptation could be classed among her
stage triumphs of the mid-to-late 1910's; and it is lamentable that
this successful stage production, like so many others during the
period, was never published for later generations to enjoy.

XI   As the Wind Blew (*1920*)

In 1932, Princess Troubetzkoy wrote to Kenneth Magruder,
who was then proposing to write her biography, that, if she

had her literary life to live over, she would do her best to excel with poetry.[21] She doubtlessly made this statement with the realization that *As the Wind Blew,* her one volume of lyrics published twelve years before, had been, on the whole, less than successful. The reviewer who generalized that her verses were written "with the left hand," [22] may have overstated the case; but he was certainly correct in several specific instances.

Appearing in the final decade of the Princess' career, *As the Wind Blew* is a selection of verses which span the preceding three and one-half decades. In general, they show the various strengths and weaknesses of these years discussed above. The combined quality, therefore, is uneven. As might be expected, the lowest level of performance is seen in the earlier poems, which are undermined both by the persistence of doggerel rhyme and by contrived archaisms similar to the ones which infused the early Romantic short stories. In "The Wonderful Child," which shows examples of both weaknesses, the Christ child is arbitrarily given hands "brown and wee" for no apparent reason except that a rhyme is needed for "see." [23] Earlier in the poem (75), the archaic past participle "gat" is unnaturally used in order to have a rhyme for "that." In "Fireflies" (15), *woken* is coined to rhyme with *spoken.*

A still more basic weakness is inappropriateness of word choice. Though not found so frequently as the above defects, it is a much more glaring offense. In one instance, the joy of a poetic heroine is "dwyning" hour by hour (31); the Christ child of "The Wonderful Child" is a "dear, douce lad." The same fault is often seen in verb endings, where an Old-Middle English *th* or *est* is inappropriately tacked onto a stem for no other apparent reason than to give the impression of a vaguely antiquated poetic diction.

For the most part, these lyrics are written in a kind of free verse, and all are charged with that romantic fancy which had lifted the early heroines of the short stories and novels above and far away from the experience of reality. For a romancer, this fancifulness can be an important gift; for a lyricist, it is often a bane. The feeling is always powerful, but its expression invariably lacks deftness. Moreover, when the free verse is used, it has a tendency to dissipate the intended emotion and to sound more like prose. For example, in the poem "Heavens," an imaginary land is discussed which is called "the place of Blueness":

There are many places in many lands of sleep
Where I have wandered wondering
Through all my life of dreaming,—
Places sweetly or terribly familiar as those of earth,
But this that I call the Place of Blueness
Is by far the loveliest and most marvellous.
Its peace is as the stillness and beings invisible
Waiting for the Great Disclosure
That shall bring fulfillment of an unimaginable beatitude
To all that was, or is, or ever shall be. (201)

Like the Princess' overall career, the poems in *As the Wind Blew* are marked by numerous examples of artistic transgression; but, just as the career is redeemed by offsetting cases of high achievement, so is the collection. There are at least three poems which might be considered masterpieces. The first of these is the prefatory elegy, "Adair," addressed to Adair Pleasants Archer, a cousin of the Princess. Like her, he had been a child prodigy, having written and starred in an operetta at fifteen. He then studied playwriting in George P. Baker's "47 Workshop" and produced a significant amount of drama and verse. Though never formally trained in painting, he was recommended for a curatorial post at the Metropolitan Museum by two Harvard professors of fine arts. Archer also shared with Princess Troubetzkoy an avid interest in the occult. Not only did he write essays on psychic phenomena, but he considered a Latin edition of the works of Paracelsus, the Swiss conjurer, his prize possession.

When Archer died at twenty-four, in the influenza epidemic of 1914, just after enlisting in the army, his death shocked the circles of Virginia and New England by whom he was well known; and it was especially traumatic for the Princess. She had regarded him as a sort of youthful soulmate who shared her interests and whose genius was comparable to her own. Never having had any children of her own, he doubtlessly filled a void in her life. The success of the elegy is due, however, in large measure to the skillful characterization of the subject, whose many-sided nature defies simple description. The poet, realizing this complexity, sees him not "as wholly this or wholly that. . . . / As some one thing [he]'ll never be. . . ." She shows him, as

[An] Ariel sad for Caliban
A seraph interested in devils,

> A Galahad who on the revels
> of Harlequin and Magdalen
> Looked with a brother's pitying ken;
> An imp, a saint, a puck, a poet,—
> Aye,—all that knew you well must know it,
> Even a pagan out and out
> In many ways, yet so devout
> In worship of the Christians' Lord,
> So faithful to his cross adored,
> That of His grace he let you die
> For others, as on Calvary
> Himself gave up his ghost for men. . . . (vii–viii)

Despite the polarities suggested by the juxtaposition of "imp" and "saint," the clear impression throughout is of youthfulness and ethereality. These feelings are supported not only by epithets like "Ariel" and "puck," but also by short couplets which give an impression of brevity and of a more nimble movement than the longer, more stately heroic couplet.

A second major area of interest is the literary-historical tradition represented by the poem. Most English poems within the elegiac genre have been deeply rooted in two traditions: the Judaeo-Christian and/or the pastoral tradition of the Greek elegists Theocritus, Bion, and Moschus. "Adair" fits into these molds no more easily than the subject himself. Pondering the spiritual destiny of this "various boy," the poet concludes: "I cannot see you, dear, indeed, / Forever harnessed in one creed [Christianity] / When all infinity's to explore!" (viii). Instead, she pictures him as part of a more general mythos: he has become a "Dear Star," his "song triumphant mounting clear . . . / Alone unto the Great Alone."

The elegy, therefore, does not espouse the Christian tradition which, say, Tennyson's *In Memoriam* did. Neither does Amélie's include any of the pastoral machinery which such poems as Milton's "Lycidas" had borrowed from the Greeks. Her elegy is, overall, free from stylization. Instead of a subject bearing the guise of a prototypal sylvan shepherd, he is a distinct individual whose intellectual curiosity had led him across the boundaries of many traditions but whose spirit has remained free to range past these and other physical boundaries.

Such a varied, individualized, not to mention ethereal, being is most difficult to depict. That the Princess saw fit to undertake the task and that by means of well-chosen image and meter she was able to succeed is ample indication that she possessed strong, if irregular, poetic talents. "Adair" stands as an original achievement in the elegiac tradition. Furthermore, it should be recognized as such by America, which has failed to produce more than half a dozen good poems of the genre.

"Whom the Gods Love," written in 1917 for the war effort, is equally good. It pays homage to those who have died in the fighting, speaks of the rewards of their sacrifice, and asks that no sadness be shown:

> Think you they would come back, they who have wrung
> The honey and the gall from life in one great hour?
> Who have been given the freedom of God's City?
> Triumphant be their dirge who were the Flower
> Of mourning England,—shame them not with pity;
> Whom the Gods love die young! die young! die young! (56)

Another poem which sounds a contemporary note is "The City Blacksmith," the only poem in the collection which has to do with social protest. The second part of the poem shows a blacksmith chiding a machine:

> No machine that ever ran
> Can shoe a horse but the hands of a man!
> And this one thing all men shall see
> Till men and horses cease to be. (18)

In terms of much of the work that was to follow, this poem is important; for the Princess saw the machine as changing life in America and as taking from it much of the integrity which the old life had contained. It made success possible for crass shopkeepers who sold cheap merchandise, and she later attacked both. "The City Blacksmith" is also a criticism of city life contrasted to country life, and the Princess, of course, preferred the latter.

In spite of uneven quality, the volume is notable because of its variety. Many short lyrics concern natural objects like fireflies or flowers; others, abstractions. One complete section, "The Wonderful Child," is actually a narrative of the early life of Christ and of how he impressed the sinful. The "Balkan Songs," a section of poems which had appeared in *Pan's Mountain,* have a quaint charm that evokes a primitive, austere feeling. Another section, "O Babylon," is an attempt to evoke the tone of a still earlier age. This effort is in many ways more interesting, perhaps because the setting is more fascinating; and, as in the Balkan songs, there is a quaint charm and childlike candor in the lines, especially in the long love poem "Belânu and Iltani."

Two other poems deserve mention. The first is "Box Hedges," in which the poet, sitting in the bedroom of her old Virginia home and gazing out the window at the boxwood bushes, is involuntarily taken away in a flight of fancy in which she sees a white unicorn by the bushes. A young woman who comes between the unicorn and the poet is Amélie at twenty-one. This poem is interesting primarily because it represents the classic case of the poet's being able to see the fanciful in the midst of the commonplace of her own experience. Both the young poet in the poem and the unicorn can be seen as psychological symbols of the poet's desire in her mid-fifties to recapture a youth now long past.

The other poem, "The Magic Tree," is clearly the most intellectually challenging in the collection. Dedicated to Amy Lowell, it contains a fine allegorical description of Miss Lowell's poetic interests. It concerns a woman who, unsatisfied by all the "trees" of life she has ever seen, decides to create her own, one

> Bearing many fruits,
> Many blossoms,
> Bearing things no other tree has borne,
> Amazing,
> Different. . . . (194)

XII *Transitions 1920–23*

At the time of the publication of *As the Wind Blew,* Princess Troubetzkoy was working on a play about Elizabeth I, to be called at different times during the next two decades "The Young Elizabeth," "The Crown of Flame," and "Bel Phoebe." In the same year, 1920, her lucrative motion picture version of *The Fear Market* appeared. The next year, her friend Emily Clark, with the help of Richmond literati Ellen Glasgow, James Branch Cabell, and Hunter Stagg established *The Reviewer,* Virginia's contribution to the horde of "little magazines" which were appearing all over the nation; and naturally the Princess was asked to contribute. Though her offerings are of minor interest, she was active in numerous background activities. She helped, for instance, with acquiring free literary contributions from well-known writers and with entertaining those authors who visited the editors. In the process, she formed numerous lifelong friendships with such figures as her distant cousin James Branch Cabell (whose *Jurgen* she and the Prince had helped defend during the famous scandal of 1920); Emily Clark; Joseph Hergeshemier; and H. L. Mencken.

In 1922, Amélie began suffering once more from neuralgia attacks; and she attempted in the early autumn of that year to get her Elizabeth play produced in London without success. The failure to produce the play and the renewed illness both indicated that the preceding years of health and busy activity were slowly ending. Her next book, *The Sea-Woman's Cloak and November Eve,* contained two experimental plays not intended for popular audiences. Only three works remained—*The Queerness of Celia, Love-in-A-Mist,* and *Firedamp*—which would receive popular acclaim, and her good health would gradually give way to bad.

XIII   The Sea-Woman's Cloak *and* November Eve (*1923*)

The Sea-Woman's Cloak, produced in the spring of 1924 by Richard Boleslawsky in his Laboratory Theatre, was the first production of the group headed by this former director of the Moscow Art Theater. He had started this theater in America in an attempt to develop new talent both in writing and in acting; and he is said to have selected the play without knowing that the author was wife of a fellow Russian immigrant. The play received favorable reviews, but most of them came from those who enjoyed the Irish patois, just as they had the Elizabethan dialect of "A Brother to Dragons." While comparing the dialect writing is certainly justified, it should not imply that the play contains any of the weaker elements of the early story. On the contrary, it is well structured; and the characters, though fantastic, are well motivated.

Having been anointed with sea water as an infant, Colum Dara, now about twenty, has grown up believing in the Irish gods who rule the sea. At the opening of the play, he is on his way to make an oblation to these deities and is accompanied by his brother

Michael, a strict and narrow Catholic who disapproves of his brother's pagan beliefs. Both brothers hear the distant cry of a sea nymph, and both step into the sea when Colum makes his offering of bread and honeyed milk; but, when Colum finds a red silk cloak and walks farther into the water to seek its supernatural owner, Michael, fearing that he will be drowned, runs in search of a priest and a rescue party.

The voice of an invisible sea goddess asks Colum for the cloak; but he, realizing that he who possesses the cloak possesses control over the owner, refuses. Though the voice warns him that looking upon a sea nymph's face will bring him sorrow, he keeps the cloak and stares into the mist until the woman becomes visible. She is Ganoré, the daughter of Lir, the Celtic counterpart of Neptune and the sister of Manannan, Prince of the Ocean. The act ends with the other nymphs calling "Woe, woe to Ganoré" [24] as she and Colum start for his mother's cottage.

The second act begins with an altercation between the widow Cathleen Dara (mother of Colum and Michael) and the strong-willed Sara Darcy, who wishes to marry Colum. The mother, opposed to this marriage, tries to explain to the girl that Colum's first love is the sea and that Sara should marry the more domestic and Christian Michael; but Sara resents her interference. When Colum and Ganoré appear at the door, the mother's reaction is surprise; Sara's is anger, and she accuses Colum of having been unfaithful to her. When the priest and some villagers arrive in response to Michael's entreaty, everyone begins questioning Ganoré. After Michael relates what has happened earlier in the evening, most of the onlookers believe Ganoré to be a real princess of the sea; but none wants her to stay except Colum. When the priest commands Colum to return the cloak to her so she may return from whence she came, he defies this rather stupid man of the cloth who in turn excommunicates him. After everyone leaves, Colum turns to Ganoré, expecting her to receive him in love. She does not, even though he reminds her that he has renounced the salvation of his soul for her. When she again asks him for her cloak and he refuses, she answers, "Free are the hearts of the sea-people ever and always!" (54). Colum reacts by picking her up and taking her into the bedroom of the cottage, where he says he will at least possess her physically. The act ends with the sea-women's voices singing her woe.

Twenty years have passed when Act III opens; and Colum is old and gray, and even Ganoré is graying. In the course of these years, she has never loved him and has refused to do all domestic chores, which he himself is left to do. She has remained spiritually free, therefore. His love has been selfish—not really love at all. He is, of course, unhappy; and she says his unhappiness was decreed on the evening she came to him. When he asks if his now much softened love should not elicit love from her, she simply answers, "How shall a prisoner believe in the love of a jailer? . . ."(62).

Then Colum's mother enters. After twenty years, she has been given a special dispensation by the Pope to see her son. Ganoré hears the voices of the other sea-women and sees three white swans (the women in disguise) pass the window. When she goes out to be with her own kind, she leaves Colum and his mother inside. He learns from her that Michael is dead—that twenty years of marriage to Sara Darcy have proved too much for him. She tells Colum of a recent dream, in which she has seen a red spot in the sky. The spot, which turns out to be the cloak, has begun coming toward her; and, as it neared, she could see him and Ganoré sitting upon it. Then a voice tells her to tell Colum to give the cloak back in order that he may end his days as a Christian. During this long speech, Ganoré has entered; and she now asks again for the cloak. When Mrs. Dara asks Ganoré if she loves Colum, she answers, "What is this loving that holds the unloving in bondage?"(73).

Before Catherine leaves, Sara Darcy arrives. Always a shrew, she has now adopted a kind of Christian arrogance. She calls Ganoré a "Fool-of-the-sea," criticizes her housekeeping, and calls her magical powers ineffectual over a Christian woman with a rosary in her pocket. Finally, Sara reveals the major reason for having come: she has just found the cloak; and, partly out of spite and partly because she thinks she may have a second chance to marry Colum, she threatens to return it to Ganoré. Colum, suddenly filled with resentment for Sara and love for Ganoré, takes the cloak and spreads it over the shoulders of the latter, saying, "But if it's triumphing you are this night, it's she shall triumph also! . . . (83). Then Ganoré, impressed that Colum has given her the cloak, says that she will now give him her love; and she invites him to share the cloak with her. When she wraps it about them both, they become young again. "Short was your triumph,"

Colum says to Sara, "but we are triumphant forever!"(84). Ganoré then invokes the gods of the sea, a flash of lightning comes, and she and Colum disappear. When another flash comes, a huge sweep of the sea comes into the cottage, at which the unbelieving Sara gives a shriek. When the wave recedes, she is lying on the floor, apparently dead.

Though not fully realized until the final scene, the theme of *The Sea-Woman's Cloak* is really paganism versus parochialism. Though visible in earlier works such as *Pan's Mountain* and *The Golden Rose*, it receives more salient treatment here, especially in the areas of love and religion. The ignorant Sara Darcy is a provincial virago in contrast to the regal, mysterious Ganoré. The Irish priest is a thick-headed idiot whose narrow interpretation of religion is repulsive to Colum. Colum, the only human character in the play with individuality, is appropriately the central figure. He has been reared with a parochial notion of Catholicism shared by the villagers as well as with a love of the mystical beauties of Celtic mythology. One is sympathetic with his choice of love and religion on the larger, more beautiful scale.

The play is not intended, however, as a denunciation of organized religion or of conventional human love; it is a condemnation of the parochial practice of each and an attempt to show that there are beautiful and ethical values which lie outside the forms which society has condoned. The play is, in short, a living manifestation of the words addressed to young Adair Archer in *As the Wind Blew:* "I cannot see you dear, indeed, / Forever harnessed in one Creed, / When all infinity's to explore!"

Setting and minor characters immediately call to mind John Millington Synge's *Riders to the Sea,* but not the language. Both plays show the Irish peasants as practitioners of a demanding organized religion but as, nevertheless, aware of the sea as an awesome supernatural force. Moreover, both plots portray the sea as part of a pagan myth which exerts its influence upon all who live upon its shores and who take their livelihood from its depths. There is, however, a notable difference in the language of the two plays. Synge is frequently cited for his faithful reproduction of the Anglicized Celtic idiom. The language of *The Sea-Woman's Cloak* is quite stylized. Sentence structure varies but seldom: the initial word is usually a contraction, followed by a predicate element. For example, when the brothers are going to make their sacrifice,

Michael yells to Colum, "It's not into the sea itself you'll have me going this night!"(17). Earlier, Colum has told Michael, " 'Tis not fish tails the sea-women have . . ."(16). Given the fact that these are peasants and that this speech pattern is popular in Ireland, the language of Synge and Sean O'Casey is customarily interspersed with the English order of subject-predicate. In other words, the dialect, while, for the most part, sounding like Celticized English, is written with a too-heavy hand; it needs discriminative selectivity instead of full force.

Amélie's *November Eve*, another Irish play, also features the theme of love and religion on two planes; but, unlike *The Sea-Woman's Cloak*, it is concerned with two interpretations of Christianity. The action takes place during a single Hallowe'en, or November Eve, a day celebrated in both the Christian and pagan worlds. The peasants in the play believe that, because the dead and the little people hold sway on this evening, one should stay inside, fortify oneself with a feast, and nail branches of rowan and ground ivy over the doorway (the latter to trip up the little people).

Years before the play opens, Bega, one of the peasants, has been brought by her stepson a strange little girl, who, he says, "was born of a day of love in the land of Heart's Desire, and it's Ilva you will call her . . ."(100). Though believing her to be part fairy, Bega has reared the child and has come to love her. On this November Eve, Ilva is absent from the dinner Bega is giving for the villagers; and all are concerned about her. She soon enters, carrying a little black lamb which she has found wandering about the village. The peasants fear the animal because it is black, but Ilva protects it simply because it is a helpless creature. Thus the two reactions to this obvious symbol of Christianity emphasize the disparity between the narrow and highly superstitious Christian love of the villagers and the far-reaching variety of it practiced by Ilva.

As the play progresses, this disparity is intensified. A wandering friar enters, seeking protection from the dead who are supposedly abroad. When Ilva suggests that a kind word should be said for the departed, the friar thinks her demented. Then a neighbor arrives with the news that Shawn Rau has murdered his adulterous wife. When Ilva asks the holy man to go to seek Shawn, he refuses, saying that he cannot leave the souls in the cottage. The remainder of the play shows Ilva's practice of charity to the downtrodden. She goes to Shawn Rau and tells him that she brings the love of Christ, who prayed for His murderers. Shawn repents, saying he would give his own life to see his wife alive again. Ior, a fairy prince, now appears to offer to take Ilva back to the supernatural realm from which she had come. She refuses on the grounds that living with him in a bond of love would be selfish, since they would show love only for each other. She has learned an all-embracing Christian love for all living beings.

She therefore decides to stay on the earth, whereupon she carries Shawn back to the cottage for the friar to hear his confession. Just after she arrives, the voice of Ior drifts in, once more tempting her to come away; but she goes out into the morning, reaches out her arms, and says, "Oh, my heart's desire! . . . Oh, the loneliness! . . ."(156). This final action indicates that once one has embarked upon the path of love for all mankind, he must follow a long, lonely route. He can look forward to self-denial and to a lack of sympathy from those whose outward promises to follow the same course are but hollow gestures.

XIV The Queerness of Celia (*1926*)

Through the mid-1920's the Princess was plagued with frequent attacks of grippe and neuralgia, as well as with diminished financial security. In 1925 she wrote her friend Ellen Glasgow, a regular correspondent during the 1920's, that she was too "poor" to pay the full fifty dollars for a life membership in the Richmond Society for the Prevention of Cruelty to Animals and could only send half.[25] In the same letter she told Miss Glasgow that she had been amusing herself by writing "a light little novel called 'The Queerness of Celia.' " The fact that she called it "light" and "little" is revealing; for it shows conclusively what has been suggested before: she was not a reliable critic of her own work. *The Queerness of Celia* is not a masterpiece, but it is certainly among the best novels she wrote.

The "queerness" of the protagonist, Celia Gibbs, is actually less a matter of strangeness than of quiet introversion that is broken occasionally by searingly frank statements. Having been left by her artist father as the ward of young Hilary Fraser, socialite and scholar, she is educated in a convent school in Brittany, as is

Fraser's niece Maud Eversham. At fourteen, Celia shocks Fraser by announcing that she has lost all faith in Catholicism. After asking for money to buy Maud a gift, she additionally surprises her guardian by explaining that she really dislikes the girl but wishes to give her the present because Maud likes her.

Even more shocking is Celia's admission that she remembers her father as a drunkard and as a harsh parent. Fraser senses a basic unhappiness behind all these statements, so he decides to attempt to make up for her hitherto traumatic existence. He arranges to have her make a debut with Maud and begins designing her clothes, and she soon regards him as infallible. Until now, she has lived with Fraser's sister; but, when she dies, he is at a loss about what to do with her. When he suggests that she accept the marriage proposal of the young Russian sculptor Kirilenko, she refuses. He thinks of establishing her in a separate household but reconsiders, realizing that it will appear that he is keeping her as a mistress. When he finally proposes a marriage of convenience, she accepts.

Neither enters into union with any thought of connubial love. He accepts her pronouncement that she will never love anyone; and he, in turn, having never offered his love to anyone, does not offer it to her. Each is content to let the other pursue individual interests: for him, research for a book on medieval art; for her, an interest in mythology and daydreaming. The two make, however, frequent social appearances together; and, during the first season following her marriage, Celia overhears two dowagers say that she has married Hilary for his money. This chance remark causes her to go to a money-hungry theatrical producer to get a job as a high-diving artist in order to prove to herself that her own abilities are sufficient for self-support. This venture is important in two ways: first, it forces her out of her habit of introspection and improves her self-confidence in the process; second, it causes Hilary to realize that "she needs love and doesn't know it . . . ,"[26] though he apparently feels none of the love he ultimately shows for her.

Before she and Hilary have the opportunity to move closer to a normal marriage relationship, Celia meets Padraic O'Shea, a young violinist. He begins an ardent courtship, which brings her increased realization of the advantages to be found in a natural love relationship. When she also realizes that Hilary has treated

her as a child, she chides him for it. Before the marriage, she and
Hilary had agreed that, if either should fall in love with someone
else, the other could terminate the union. She and O'Shea plan to
elope, thus giving Hilary grounds for divorce based upon deser-
tion. In preparing for the elopement, Celia buys a new outfit that
is quite different from anything Hilary had ever designed for her.
Then she has her long ashen hair cut so short that she looks boyish. When O'Shea meets her on the train, he fails to recognize her
at first. When he realizes that it is she, he is barely able to conceal
his unhappiness over the new outfit and hair-style. Celia senses his
reaction; and, while he goes to the club car to rethink his decision
over a drink, she writes him a farewell note, stating that they have
both made a big mistake.

She gets off at the next stop, wanders about aimlessly for some
while, and thoughtlessly wanders into an empty house. There,
while trying to unscramble her now tangled existence, she sees an
unvarnished picture of herself for the first time in her life. This
likeness is of someone undeserving, rude, and spiteful. The image
likewise calls to mind her father, and for the first time she is confronted with the question of who she really is. The answer is simple: she is her father's daughter. As such, she is little better than
the man whose memory she has castigated for so many years.
Moreover, she has never really known love; and now she fears
that her actions may have prevented her from ever receiving it
from the one man who most logically might have shown it had she
been receptive: Hilary Fraser. She returns to him a true penitent,
stating, "I've fallen too low . . . ever to get up. . . . Please . . .
please say you forgive . . ."(304). Though inexperienced in
matters of love, Hilary realizes that he loves her and tells her so.

Celia offers more opportunity for psychological investigation
than any Rives heroine before or after. Especially is this true in
the final quarter of the book after she has begun to emerge from
the introspective shell which had inhibited her actions in earlier
scenes. The cutting of her hair, for instance, has important psychological implications. Hair is a common symbol of sexuality, but
Celia has hers cut just before embarking on the elopement which
would bring her sexual fulfillment. This action is underscored by
the fact that she has always wanted to wear boyish ties and
blouses (254). Both facts clearly indicate that she is unsure of her
sexual identity and naïve about how she should go about estab-

lishing it. This supposition is confirmed by O'Shea's reaction to her
new appearance: he is repulsed by it. Obviously, he had sensed
her sexual attractiveness as demonstrated by her hair; its absence
has obscured the identity of the sexual object.

In a larger psychological sense, Celia passes through the three
classic stages of the archetypal initiation pattern: separation,
transformation, and return. Though daily in the presence of
Hilary Fraser, she has learned no more of love from her relationship with him than she had from her father. Neither does she
learn anything about the subject from her associations with
O'Shea. It is only in her separation from these men that her transformation occurs. The return, or final stage in the cycle, shows her
ready for love now that she realizes that her own headstrong ways
have been the major cause of its absence.

Though this psychological development is not seen until late in
the story, it stands out as an uncommon feature in the Princess'
work. With the exception of Phoebe Nelson and Barbara Dering,
all other heroines are essentially static characters. Celia Gibbs indicates that the author was able to create another kinetic heroine
and that she understood the psychological implications of her
character's development. Moreover, it is rather refreshing to see a
heroine who has some shortcomings and inadequacies. Former
Rives heroines were often dignified and occasionally even noble
creatures, but they seldom showed weaknesses of the sort which
complicate Celia's life.

Like Phoebe Nelson, Tanis Gribble, and Trix Bruce, Celia is
obviously not modeled upon her creator. Elsewhere in the story,
however, one finds several instances of thinly disguised autobiographical experience. The obvious example is Celia's encounter
with Abel Sieburg, the aggressive theatrical manager who hires
her as a high-dive artist because she has "class." The excessive
length of the scene and the attention given to the repulsive attitude of the producer make it safe to assume that the Princess herself was forced to deal with such people during the war years and
after. A similar instance is the episode between Celia, the sales-
girl, and the shopkeeper from whom she buys her boyish trous-
seau. These characters are every bit as greedy and crass as
Sieburg.

Collectively, such scenes appear as commentaries on the post-
World War I economic boom in America. It is obvious that these

conditions rankled the sensibilities of the Princess, whose values
were shaped in a politer Victorian era. Yet, in the one occasion
when direct authorial comment is made, it is directed at the sanctimonious Prohibition Act. When O'Shea is drinking his glass of
Scotch, the Princess wryly comments that "In those days America
was still more or less 'the land of the free!' not the sanctimonious
reformatory which it is fast becoming"(279–80). It was obvious
that the 1920's represented far from the best of possible worlds
and that the old critical fire was still burning.

XV   Love-in-A-Mist (*1927*)

The favorably reviewed *Queerness of Celia* was followed the
next year (1927) with *Love-in-A-Mist*, the only successful com-
mercial play by the Princess Troubetzkoy to be published after
its Broadway run. Written in collaboration with Gilbert Emery
(whose real name was Emery Bemsley Pottle), the play was described by young Joseph Wood Krutch as "a thoroughly amusing
farce written with brightness and speed . . . and given sufficient
depth of characterization almost to constitute it a comedy. . . ." [27]
The basis for Krutch's remark about depth of characterization was
probably the part of the heroine, Diana Wynne, whose dislike for
unpleasant truths has given her an unfortunate penchant for
lying.

The action centers around a long series of her lies. The first is a
false confession of love to Count Scipione Varelli, made before
the play opens, when she has heard that he is dying and wishes
him to do so happily. The second is another profession of love
made to an unnamed young man threatening suicide if he does not
hear it. She performs this unfortunate service while engaged to
Gregory Farnham who, taking the fib for the truth, sets out with a
broken heart on an expedition to Asia. The play opens just as he
returns to a repentant Diana, who tells him that she is currently
unattached and that she has lied to save the young man's life.

But still other lies are made necessary when "Scippi" Varelli
appears. She tries to escape the consequences of the lie she has told
him before the play opens by more lying: she must leave immediately for Washington to see her ailing mother. But Scippi blandly
announces that he has just seen her mother and that she is in the
pink of health. Gregory, who immediately sees through this at-

tempted falsehood, asks her for a candid account of her relationship with Scippi. Though the simple truth might easily rectify the
situation, Diana, fearing unpleasantness, fibs once more by saying
that Scippi is really in love with her sister Sydney Rose. She even
indignantly upbraids Gregory for insinuating that she is a liar.

Then Scippi, who has been whisked off to bed, comes in; and,
while he and Gregory have a drink together, they begin talking
rather amiably. When Gregory, half believing what Diana has
told him about Scippi and Sydney Rose, refers to their engagement, Scippi answers that such cannot be the case for he and
Diana are engaged. When Diana enters and when Gregory demands the truth, she tells it for once—that she has expressed her
love to Scippi out of sympathy. As she feared, the results are dis-
astrous. Scippi rushes out, and in a moment a shot is heard: he has
tried to take his life. Act II ends with Diana's mournful statement,
"you see what happens when I tell the truth!"

This incident is the height of the complication, and it creates a
serious atmosphere. To lie in a comic context can be funny; but,
when serious consequences such as attempted suicide occur, the
situation is anything but amusing. However, from this point on,
comedy is dominant; but it is comedy with a message—one never
intense enough to destroy the humor but sufficient to temper it
from its high pitch of the first and second acts. During the three
weeks which separate the second and third acts, Gregory aban-
dons Diana. She, in the meantime, has gone to Washington to be
with Scippi's mother. Scippi has been slowly recuperating and is
brought downstairs for the first time during this act. When he
comes down, he, Sydney Rose, Anna Moore, and the servants go
into the garden.

Just then, Diana arrives, having been sent for by Anna Moore;
and, quite by coincidence, Gregory enters at the same time. He
believes that she has arranged the meeting; and, when she says
she hasn't, he takes her declaration to be another lie. When Anna
Moore takes Gregory into the garden, and Sydney Rose and
Scippi are left alone, Scippi has a fine opportunity to tell Sydney
that he loves her and that he wishes to marry her. Then Sydney is
summoned to the garden, Scippi is left alone, and Diana enters.
For the last time in the play she tells what she believes to be a
well-intended fib: she tells Scippi she has been in love with him
all along. When the others come in, Diana announces her love;

and Scippi becomes distraught. Gregory makes Diana promise
that she will never lie to Scippi because he is a good person who
deserves better treatment. This speech elicits a final confession
from Diana that her previous statement has been a lie: "I have
always lied for the best—even if it didn't turn out that way—and
that's what I've done now. No decent girl could have done anything else. I'm doing a better thing now than I have ever done
before!" [28] Gregory's final comment is, "Your heart's all right, God
bless it! But, oh, God damn your head!"(96). Just then Sydney
Rose and Scippi come in, and he is professing his love for her.
Diana then turns happily to Gregory, and the play ends with his
threats against further lying.

One of the most remarkable aspects, besides the heroine, is the
satiric realism found in this comedy of manners. Reference is
made to Prohibition, to sex, and to the manners of the rich of the
day. There are also a number of caricatures, such as protective
Aunt Anna Moore, who is somewhat slow-witted; numerous
comic servants; and the typical stage Italian, Scippi. Diana
Wynne is a delightful study of a girl's interpretation of morals:
her concept of truth and falsehood depends upon whether or not
a pleasant social situation results. She is not amoral, but she has
no concept of the value of truth. The lines are witty; the action
moves swiftly; the structure is well conceived. The infusion of the
moral tone in the last act was one of the most difficult parts of the
play to achieve, but it is accomplished without injecting too much
didacticism.

Love-in-A-Mist, like *The Queerness of Celia* which had appeared the year before, was truly a literary work forged out of
contemporary materials. Not only are both set in the age in which
they appeared, but both contain important comments about aspects of the era: Prohibition was hypocritical; sex could be fit
topic for conversation; people should be whole in themselves and
not worry about the way others thought and acted; aristocracy
and riffraff still very much existed, and the former was preferable.

All these comments are significant insights into the 1920's, and
they are views shared by many. What is so outstanding is that
they were made by a woman in her sixties, but then she had been
regarded as a rebellious maiden of the late Victorian era. Earlier
in the 1920's she had discussed with her friend Emily Clark a review of *As the Wind Blew* which had appeared in the British

Saturday Review and which had compared her to G. K. Chesterton. "They write of Chesterton," she told Miss Clark, "as a settled
author, while of me they speak as though I were a giddy young
thing full of promise if I'd only stick to my last of modernity!
Could unconscious flattery go further? For Mr. Chesterton is at
least twelve or fourteen years older than I am and has a capari-
soned, war-horse, Roman Catholic mind, while I shall be sixty
next August and my wits are still unsaddled and uncertain." [29] This
remark is significant not only because the Princess was almost
sixty when she made it but because, in the four books she was to
publish thereafter, her wits were still "unsaddled and uncertain."
One is unaware that *The Queerness of Celia* or *Love-in-A-Mist*
are by a woman in her mid-sixties, or that *Firedamp* (1930), her
last book, was written later in the same decade of her life. Still the
Princess was able to benefit from her age, for it had brought the
maturity reflected throughout the works of the second period.

XVI   Firedamp (*1930*)

Firedamp is lively and vigorous enough to have been written by
a writer in his thirties, but it is quite mature and may be numbered among the five best novels the Princess ever wrote. Above
all, there is no indication whatever in the book or among the
Princess' papers that it was ever intended to be her final work;
and it is no more a final statement than was *Shadows of Flames*.
As in some of her previous books, the plot develops from a
Jamesian situation: an American woman (a Virginian) is abroad
among a British society which is anything but innocent. But, unlike much of her previous fiction, a male character has equal
prominence with the heroine.

This character, Victor Glyndon, is a young Briton who serves
with the Foreign Service in Rome. He aspires to leave the service
to follow his literary inclinations, which are considerable; for he
has already written one novel and, as the story opens, has just
received word that his London agent likes his new play, *Odd-
ments*. Victor, who has been ill, is about to return to England for
a leave. When he gets to his family's ancestral home, Glyndon
Hall, he finds all the members of the family he had anticipated:
his older brother Bob (the future Lord Glyndon); his mother,
Matoaka (the former Matoaka Carey from Virginia); Ronny

Glyndon, his young lawyer cousin; Hilda Purfitt, a young lady in love with Ronny; and finally Lord Glyndon, Victor's seventy-year-old father, who dislikes Victor as much as he dislikes his father. As the homecoming progresses, it is discovered that Blair Van Ryn, a cousin of Matoaka from Virginia, is a house guest.

Victor's stay is to be quite important in the lives of all these characters. The enmity between him and his father reasserts itself and grows; he and Blair fall in love (though they do not profess it until much later); the affection between Hilda and Ronny reaches a crisis (he temporarily refuses to marry her and be "kept" by her fortune); and, most importantly, Bob admits to Victor that he has cancer. Although Victor has resolved to quit the Foreign Service, he hesitates to tell his father, who has a volatile nature and who calls him names like "foreigner." For reasons later explained, Lord Glyndon resents Victor, so he and Bob finally decide that he had better return to Rome to keep their father reasonably quiet. Also, it will seem natural for him to do so; for, if he stayed at Glyndon Hall, questions might be asked which would reveal Bob's illness, which he wishes to remain a secret.

Both sons love their mother far more than their father, for she is gentle and compassionate; he, vile and corrupt. One is given the impression that, if he is this way by nature, he doesn't care that he is when, late in the novel, he declares to his sister Emily (who is almost as vile as he), "My philosophy is the same as Peacock's. [He is a lover of Gothic romances, especially Peacock's *Nightmare Abbey* and Beckford's *Vathek*, which he thinks better than *Hamlet*.] With him I consider life a farce, and he who laughs most has most profit of the performance. I have a vile temper, as you know, but even that failing has its saving grace. Irritating trivialities move me to violence. Graver matters, even when they are most irritating, congeal me. . . ." [30]

However, there is a haunting memory which from time to time is suggested to Victor, though it is not explained until late in the story, which explains in part old Glyndon's attitude. Victor is reminded sporadically of a Colonel Varnall who had been his commanding officer in World War I. The Colonel was mortally wounded while saving Victor's life; and, as he died in delirium, he told Victor that he was really his father. But the fact that Victor has never held any resentment for his mother and that she has been able to hold her head high in the ensuing years tes-

tify to the depth of her character. It is somewhat to her justification in having done what she did that, when the full truth is found
out, she had planned to leave her tyrannical husband, who had
continually kept mistresses, for the man she had really loved and
had planned to marry. His death in the war has caused her to live
in a hell composed of her hateful husband and of his knowledge
of her action, which he holds over her.

The brothers have decided that Victor is to stay in Rome until
Bob's condition worsens; then he is to resign and return home to
be with Bob and their mother. On his way to Rome, Victor stops
in London for a few days to check on the progress of his play and
is gratified to find that it is to be produced. Another incident
greatly upsets him, however. Hilda, believing that Ronny has
jilted her, has begun seeing Tisford Luttrall, a decadent young
novelist. Victor decides to intercede for Ronny, who by this time
has almost agreed to marry Hilda. After Victor succeeds in convincing Hilda to accept Blair's invitation for a trip through the
American West, he heads for Rome; but he and Blair correspond
from time to time. She aspires to become an actress and wants to
play the part of Gloria in his play should it be presented in the
United States; and one of her most encouraging letters reports
that Winterleigh, an American theatrical producer, has consented
to produce it.

Before long, Victor is summoned home; Bob is worse. Though
the two have some fine days of sailing in the late summer, Bob
gradually weakens and finally dies in December. He has made his
father promise that he will be kind to Victor; but, after he is gone,
old Glyndon makes only futile attempts at civility. Victor feels
uncomfortable around him, and his mother is not sufficiently recovered from her nervous collapse after Robert's death to come
down to meals. The uncomfortable situation is relieved by news
from Blair that her divorce from Harold Van Ryn, a collector of
Italian primitives and a man many years older than she, is now
final. Victor writes her of his love and sails for America. After
stopping in New York to see Winterleigh and the proposed director of the play, Neville Orme, he immediately goes to Uplands,
the Castle Hill antitype in the story and the Virginia home of
Victor's mother's family, where Blair lives with her cousin Ed-
wina, or "Ted." While in the womblike surrounding which the
plantation always provides in the Princess' stories, word comes

from Winterleigh that Blair has been selected to play the part of Gloria.

In a few days Victor and Blair are in New York to prepare for the play. As in *The Queerness of Celia,* there are many adverse criticisms of the theatrical world. Orme is shown to be an unfeeling, tyrannical director—unyielding and crude. One of the actors is portrayed as effeminate and childish. After a hot exchange with Orme, Victor becomes the director (he tells Winterleigh that he has watched Pirandello rehearse actors and that he will use his techniques). The play is quite successful. Blair drops out of her role in June to marry Victor, and they immediately leave for England.

They have received a letter from Lord Glyndon but are wary of his cordiality. He is simply never pleasant unless he is riding a victim for a fall. He has just had a stroke, brought on by a fit of anger; and he knows that another fit could kill him. All seem concerned by his affability, even Ronny and Hilda, who have just been married. After dinner on the night of Victor and Blair's arrival, old Glyndon sends for Victor and his mother to tell them that he has collected all the information possible to prove that Victor is not his real son so that he will not be able to succeed to his title and lands. What is worse, he has told his sister of the facts to insure that the information will get into the right hands. When the old man begins talking, Victor claps his hand over his mouth and asks his mother to leave, which she dutifully does. Then he leaves, followed by a spate of profanity, indicating his illegitimacy, from Glyndon. Matoaka is, of course, brokenhearted by her husband's vindictiveness; but Victor consoles her, telling her that he has known the truth since the war.

When word comes that Lord Glyndon has apparently had another stroke and is dead, Victor grabs the envelope which contains the information and locks it in his room. But soon, Emily, hysterical that the papers be found (they will give the title to her son Ronny), tells Ronny. Matoaka, in her most magnificent scene, goes to Emily to tell her that Ronny will be given the papers. Victor is naturally willing to accept the situation, but he does not want his mother's name smeared. Ronny nobly offers to resign the title (which will mean that no one may claim it during his lifetime) and to live at Glyndon if Victor wishes. What is most important, however, is that the real truth will not be made public.

Victor, thoroughly shaken, goes outside with Blair and, lying down on a pile of hay in a nearby field, drops "into a sleep as a stone drops into a well"(344).

Considering the novel's glittering cast of characters, it is fitting that it should be narrated from the omniscient point of view; but there is negligible authorial intrusion. The narrative shows fine control in that the characters are sufficiently portrayed to speak for themselves. The story was not an easy one to tell, for much background is needed. It is, however, skillfully supplied through the recurring memory of Victor and finally by the confrontation between old Glyndon and Matoaka, so that the narrative is enhanced and not encumbered.

Moreover, there is commentary on the era which is unsurpassed by that in any of the Princess' previous books. Vestiges of Victorianism and its frequent sentimentality are derisively portrayed. For example, Hilda's mother is described as a "pretty die-away woman" (108) who had been a pale flower compared to her pragmatic husband, a man of the world whom Hilda strongly resembles. A song, "The Tree of Life," is dismissed as "1890 and sentimental"(269). In short, there seems to be a respect for a Realistic approach to life, as opposed to a Romantic one. Yet this Realism did not mean that the Princess had abandoned the imaginative. For example, Blair's letter to Victor admits, "I'm afraid we have shamelessly romantic notions for this sharpcut, disillusioned age. You being a man may cast them out in time. But I'm quite hopeless. I like illusions. I encourage them. I even made a little prayer for myself once, which I still say, 'Lord, I thank thee for my pleasant illusions!'—That will show you I am beyond redemption—the fact, I mean, that I say prayers at all, let alone such a prayer! . . ." (177). The sentimentality and the unbridled style which made hearts soar instead of beat and tears gush instead of run have disappeared. Still the old feeling for the world and the creatures which inhabit it is present and continues to be so.

A brief word is in order concerning the title, which is rather cryptic and which is never mentioned in the text. It indicates the reconciling of the opposites of fire (his love) and dampness in Victor's life (his experience with his father). His peaceful sleep beside his wife at the end of the book indicates that the two opposites have become reconciled and that his life is thereby unified.

The Princess combines these opposites in the title to indicate the poignance of having them together in the same story or life.

When *Firedamp* appeared in February, 1930, it was followed by such reviews as the one in the New York *Times* which, while pointing to occasional lags in plot, praised "the highly dramatic, human experiences of the Glyndons . . . [for] creating . . . a most absorbing story." [31] By this time the depression was four months old, and the inroads that it had made on the Troubetzkoys' prosperity were soon obvious. An American public, worried about getting enough food to sustain itself, could ill afford the luxury of portraits and fiction. To make matters worse, attacks of the Princess' neuralgia began once more. In December, the Prince had to write Professor John Calvin Metcalfe at the University of Virginia that illness prevented his wife from writing anything for the centennial celebration at the university.[32] The next year she was saddened both by the deaths of her close friends Louisa Pleasants and Bridgett Guinness and by her own continuing illness. The uncertainty of her health forced her to write Professor James Southall Wilson that she would be unable to attend the Southern Writers' Conference at the university,[33] but she was much pleased when a large number of the writers paid her a visit.

Hard times and ill health continued. On October 24, 1932, she wrote her cousin Rosalie Archer about being "so hard hit" by the depression that "but for the real *miracle* of Pierre's getting some orders I do not know what we should have done." [34] Her frequent attacks of neuralgia were joined by uticaria in 1933, her first attack since her twenty-eighth year (she was now seventy). In 1935 she was beset with a four-month siege of jaundice. Writing her friend Ellen Glasgow in August of that year, she thanked her for sending a copy of her new novel *Vein of Iron*, which she said she liked for the compassion it showed "for all that suffers and strives." [35] She was able, nevertheless, to manage the affairs of the farm, which were made even more difficult than usual by the shortage of labor and by the low prices paid for crops.

Through all these trials, life at Castle Hill continued, but in an altered fashion. Then, on August 25, 1936, the Prince died suddenly of angina pectoris, a disease which no one had suspected he had. The shock to the Princess was overwhelming. After his dying

in her arms, she took to her room, which she was unable to leave
for weeks. She was not even able to look on the next day as a farm
wagon drawn by two white horses bore the coffin to the Rives
plot, where it was buried one space away from Senator William
Cabell Rives. Nor was she able to hear the words of the Reverend
Francis Leslie Robinson, the rector of nearby Grace Church, who
had preached Chanler's funeral service the year before.

It was December 15 before she was able to acknowledge the
condolences of Ellen Glasgow.[36] After describing the Prince's
death, she stated what was then the comforting fact that she
would be seventy-four on her next birthday and that she would
soon join Pierre. Still sensing this consolation, she made a draft of
her will the next month in which she revealed that she had been
too ill to walk the few hundred feet from the house to Pierre's
grave. She was to rally during 1937, however, and in a letter to
Ellen Glasgow of August 25, exactly one year after the Prince's
death, she revealed not only a rationalization of the trauma, but
one of the most remarkable displays of her spirit on record. "My
chief consolation," she wrote Miss Glasgow, "has been, 'I am bearing this in Pierre's stead.' And my prayer has been to be unselfish
and to think of others more than of myself." [37] Later in the letter
she says, "I have been in that fire [that tries gold] constantly during all this interminable year and at last, by a miracle of love I
have come out of it (though I reenter it often) 'tried,' 'fined,'—the
thing that Dante meant by 'affino.' " Two weeks later she showed
another sure sign of recovery by writing Miss Glasgow to describe
in endless pages of detail the complicated beauty ritual which she
still performed each day.[38]

XVII   *The Lamp Still Shines: 1938–45*

At the end of December, 1937, and during January, 1938, Caro-
lyn Martin, a cousin, was staying at Castle Hill with the Princess
while her sister Landon Rives was away on a cruise; and the letters she wrote to Landon were generally optimistic about the
Princess' health and, more importantly, her work. By December
31, the Princess had resumed work on *The Young Elizabeth* and
was writing the conclusion of the fourth and final act. Miss Martin, a perceptive critic, as well as a pleasant companion, reported
in a letter of December 31 that she had convinced the Princess

that the act—and the play—should end with Elizabeth's words, "I am England" and be followed by no action. "All the rest of the rewritten last act is splendid," she reported; "and it really ought to thrill her to find that at her age, and with all she's been thro' the lamp still shines." [39]

The Young Elizabeth was the last work of any consequence which the Princess attempted. She had actually been revising it for some twenty years, but for various reasons she had never put the play into final form or succeeded in contracting for either production or publication. Agents were high in its praise, as was her friend Harley Granville-Barker; but there had been no impetus to complete the final polishing. Now, with the worries of the depression somewhat abated, and the death of her husband rationalized as well as possible, the seventy-four-year-old author could give her full attention to the play which concerned "the Love-story of Elizabeth Tudor and Robert Dudley, when they were young, according to legend, not to history." [40]

This time she was to meet with more success: the play was produced in the spring of 1938 by the Little Theatre of St. Louis; it was never published, though, much to the loss of the reading public. Those whose knowledge of Elizabeth I derives only from Maxwell Anderson's *Elizabeth The Queen* (1930) should read this drama. Anderson's play shows the Queen four years before her death; *The Young Elizabeth* shows her young and in love—before she had hardened into the character that Anderson presents. The youthful Elizabeth portrayed in the Princess' drama has many facets one of which is craftiness. When Queen Mary is seriously ill, she sends a spy to gauge her sister's reaction. Elizabeth's feigned sorrow is so convincing that he thinks her genuinely grieved and unconcerned about assuming the throne. Her temper is described in the *dramatis personae* as being "as fiery as her hair, and her regret for its indulgence as quick as her outbursts." This quality is shown especially well in her anger toward Mary Sidney, Dudley's sister, at whom she rails unmercifully one minute and calls endearing names the next. A lighter facet of her nature is revealed when, after naming Sir William Cecil to guide her reign, she gathers up her skirts and dances. She is also compassionate, popping a sweetmeat into the mouth of a servant whom she has tongue-lashed.

Doubtlessly, the Princess saw her own youth paralleled in Elizabeth's. She may have also seen a similarity between her former heroines and the young Queen who has been in love with Dudley (or Leicester) since childhood. In terms of nobility of character, of devotion to principle, of fire and energy, and of capability of being a strong foil to a male of weaker, more selfish nature, the Elizabeth of this play represents a crystallization of all the Princess' feminine protagonists. She is especially close to later heroines, such as Matoaka Glyndon, who are forced to resolve the painful dilemma between love and duty.

In *The Young Elizabeth,* the Princess shows, since the time that Elizabeth and Dudley had acted in St. George plays, Elizabeth has been in love with him. This love has grown during the time that both were imprisoned in the Tower of London for treason. During the reign of Mary she has not been free to marry the Protestant Dudley, nor can she do so now that she is queen because too much conflict still exists between Protestants and Catholics in England and because Dudley still has a wife. There is some glimmering of hope, nevertheless, as Amy Dudley has a "canker of the breast" which is expected to take her life at any time. When she dies, Dudley will be free to marry the Queen—if all else is well in the kingdom. Pressure has been brought to bear on the Queen by Quadra, the Bishop of Aquila, who is the representative of Philip II of Spain, the husband of the deceased Queen Mary, to marry Archduke Charles of Austria, who would bring Catholicism back to England on an equal footing with Protestantism. She, of course, does not wish to marry this dwarf.

Dudley, a proud man, has so many enemies that the Queen is afraid to give him any position higher than Master of the Horse at the beginning of her reign. And his pride, as much as his Protestantism, causes the wicked Quadra to begin rumors among Roman Catholics that Dudley plans to murder his wife so that he may marry the Queen. When his demented wife dies by suicide, he is free to marry Elizabeth; but there are still impediments. Realizing that Dudley is free, Elizabeth's womanly side takes control of the queenly one; and, amidst all the vile rumors of Dudley's intentions, she tells Sir Nicholas Throgmorton, her ambassador to France, "I am for him against all the world" (Act III, 5). During the investigation which Dudley makes into his wife's death, a maid tells that Amy Dudley's death was caused by suicide. When this information clears Dudley's name, Elizabeth makes him the highest nobleman in the realm: Earl of Leicester. But she is unsuccessful in placating the Catholic faction, even though she confesses to Quadra; therefore, she tells Dudley that the marriage will have to wait because she puts the welfare of England before her own. When Dudley protests, she answers: "The Queen made sure of her kingdom's peace. It is the woman loves you" (Act III, 25). And she is enough a diplomat to get him to fight with her against the dissenters by telling him that they fight for their happiness.

They are unsuccessful. In the end, it is impossible to reconcile the marriage with the various religious factions, and the woman-queen conflict is brought into even sharper focus. Dudley's love is selfish, and she tells him that he has forgotten England. His answer is, "It is you come first for me,—then England!" Her classic reply, which ends the play is "I am England!" The point seems more convincing than in any other drama concerning Elizabeth I, for the author has depicted a conscientious queen and a woman in love.

In characterization, language, and plot there is a naturalness which may be compared to similar aspects of Shakespeare, as pointed out by Samuel Johnson. "Shakespeare has no heroes," wrote Johnson; "his scenes are occupied only by men, who act and speak as the reader thinks that he should himself have spoken or acted on the same occasion. . . ." [41] The same may be said for the protagonist of *The Young Elizabeth*. She is not an imperious monarch but a woman in love whose emotional happiness is offset by the obligations of patriotism. To see Elizabeth torn between private happiness and public commitment is to show her in a predicament faced by many an average person. Because one does not have to be a monarch to become embroiled in such a conflict, Elizabeth's actions and conflicts have universal significance. What, though, of her words? The language of the play is prose—a wise choice over poetry which, because of intrinsic prosodic values, might detract from the denotative power of the dialogue. Elizabeth's language is neither stylized nor sensational; instead, it is "evidently determined by the incident which produces it," (63) to quote Johnson once more.

Besides being well correlated to character and action, the dialogue develops naturally to form what Johnson called a smooth "progress of [the] fable" (62) or plot. The unnatural twistings and turnings of less skillful efforts are absent here. From the opening scene, one is aware of the central conflict, and the plot moves steadily toward its resolution. There is a good reason why *The Young Elizabeth* contains this polished naturalness, which the earlier works but approximate in varying degrees; it can be summarized by a single word: revision. The manuscript of the play exists in at least half a dozen states, and numerous manuscript pages contain additional revisions of individual speeches and scenes. While the manuscripts of few other works have survived, all of the others give a similar impression of scant revision. Moreover, the Princess' nature was to give free reign to inspiration and not to fret over the refinement of initial conception.

The Young Elizabeth thus leaves one with mixed emotions. One can see by the play what careful revision might have achieved in other hastily written titles. On the other hand, one must marvel at the brilliance of her inspired first thoughts and at her ability to put them into acceptable, if not always perfected, form in a single writing. One fact is certain: one does not change the nature of an artist. To wish for possible revision in earlier works would have been as futile at the time of their composition as it is now. And rigorous revision, had it been forced upon her, might have dulled the spontaneity of her inventiveness and spoiled the freshness which she was able to maintain throughout her career.

XVIII *Recessional*

The Young Elizabeth was Princess Troubetzkoy's only significant effort after *Firedamp* (1930) before her death; and, among the few other works, only an occasional sonnet or a lyric deserves mention. It was an unhappy, disillusioned period toward the end; for the four years of World War II paralleled the final four years of her life. For years—ever since the beginning of World War I—she had mourned the passing of old-world values and more specifically of the England which she had known as a young bride. But she rallied in World War II to the cause of the British. In "Great Britain: October, 1940," a poem published in the *Western Independent* of Plymouth, England, she said that Britain could rightly be called "great" because her pride was being maintained by such brave fighting men:

> These are the people, this the foremost race,
> The crown of Man's endeavor on the earth.
> I am very humbly proud that in my veins
> Flows life from this great fount that I can say
> From England and from Scotland came the men
> And women of my house. These are the people
> Who have restored to human dignity
> Its rightful place, who by their suffering
> And scorn of it stand higher than the angels.

Two years later, stricken with rheumatic fever and very ill, she wrote Ellen Glasgow that all beings seemed fighters. "As for man becoming civilized," she continued, "—my doubt of that is one of my worst sufferings. . . . This world, despite all its beauty, has become hateful to me, and I long to leave it. . . ." [42] As the war wore on, she declined; and by mid-1944 she was nearly blind. Confined to her room, she still wrote frequent checks for birdseed and listened to the radio for music and war news. During the winter of 1944 she was taken to a nursing home in Charlottesville where few were admitted to see the tiny form which disease had reduced to eighty pounds, but which still appeared radiant, the hair shining from the several hundred strokes which it was still given each morning. When she died on June 16, 1945, she was returned to the family burial plot at Castle Hill and placed between Senator William Cabell Rives and Prince Troubetzkoy.

CHAPTER *6*

A Princess Remembered

AFTER citing her youthful beauty and her marriage to two prominent men, Princess Troubetzkoy's obituary notices attempted to discuss her literary career. Not surprisingly, *The Quick or the Dead?* was the focal point of consideration, especially the public scandal it had caused and the large sales it had enjoyed. Some writers included the anonymous publication of "A Brother to Dragons" and the author's subsequent rise to fame. Few went so far as to mention works of the second period; and, in the rare instances that any were included, titles were simply listed without explanation.

To present the case fairly requires that both artistic periods be presented and that significant contrasts between the two be pointed out. Yet, at the end of such an enterprise, one finds at best a checkered impression. When Princess Troubetzkoy announced just before her sixtieth birthday that her wits were "still unsaddled and uncertain," [1] she unwittingly testified to a career which was both diversified and uneven. A summary of the more constant features of both the artist and her work, seems, therefore, in order.

As much of the foregoing chapters has been given to a discussion of the weaknesses which characterized the Princess' earliest work and which were repeated with decreasing frequency as she progressed, it is well that these begin the discussion. These faults can be rather accurately summarized by John Ruskin's theory of the "pathetic fallacy." According to Ruskin, all writers "who feel strongly, think weakly, and see untruly" [2] belong to the "second order." Numerous titles from the earlier period make Princess Troubetzkoy a prime candidate for this category. She, like the writers cited by Ruskin, seemed unable to speak of the sea without references to "raging waves," "remorseless floods," or "raven billows" (160). Though the strong feeling for her subjects might have been justified, her overwrought expression showed the weakness of thought and the falsity of vision associated with the "pathetic fallacy."

Her literary achievements are more difficult to summarize. It is true that in the later, more Realistic, period of her work she earned a place among what Ruskin termed the "first order" of writers—those who avoided the "pathetic fallacy" by demonstrating an ability to "feel strongly, think strongly, and see truly" (159). In such works as *World's End, Shadows of Flames, Firedamp,* and *The Young Elizabeth,* she showed an accuracy of thought and vision which restrained and controlled the customary strong feeling. And, while Ruskin's foremost category shows only that one has learned to evoke feeling effectively, it likewise shows, in Princess Troubetzkoy's case, the ability to grow—a capacity lacking in many writers.

A more constant feature of both the Princess and her work is independence. The primary example is *The Quick or the Dead?,* which is usually cited for voluminous sales and its alleged prurience. More important, however, the novel was written by a naïve young woman—and a southern one at that. At the time when both male and female writers of her region were perpetuating the "moonlight and magnolia" school of fiction—and nine years before Ellen Glasgow, supposedly the most famous truant of that school, had published her first novel (anonymously)—Amélie Rives showed her independence by writing *The Quick or the Dead?*

Seléné likewise reflects this independence, as it represents an important milestone in the Esthete movement in America. In this connection, one is reminded of the lines from Gilbert and Sullivan's *Patience,* the operetta on Estheticism which brought Oscar Wilde to America in 1882. Early in the libretto, the character Bunthorne promises: "Though the Philistines may jostle, you will rank as an Apostle in the high Aesthetic band, / If you walk down Piccadilly with a poppy or a lily in your Mediaeval hand." [3] Few American writers—excepting the "flower children" of the 1960's—have walked down American streets in such a fashion, and still fewer through the avenues of American literature. Even allowing for exceptions like Poe and Whitman in the nineteenth century and the Princess' cousin James Branch Cabell in the twentieth, Estheticism has never been a major trend. However, names like Poe, Whitman, and Cabell are not easily gainsaid; and to see them

purely in terms of their endeavors in this vein is to acknowledge a
certain prominence of the movement in America. The Princess is
an important link between Whitman and Cabell, primarily because of *Seléné*, a work as exotic, as rarefied, and as decadent as
any of the other Esthetes' work, English or American.

While *The Quick or the Dead?* was written as part of the developing Realistic movement, and is thus identified with a national
trend, *Seléné* was written at a time when American readers were
being confronted with the severities of literary Naturalism. The
depressing strivings of, say, Theodore Dreiser's Sister Carrie or
the animalistic traits of Frank Norris's protagonists in *McTeague*
are a far cry from the ethereal world of Greek myth portrayed in
the poem. What the poem tells of the artist, then, is that she was
able to follow an independent artistic code and that she was not
swayed by current trends if she found them distasteful.

Fortunately, during much of her career, she did not have to rely
on her pen for a livelihood; and she was thus permitted to write
what she pleased, even though her preferences often ran counter
to those of the public. Quite by coincidence, the growing Realistic
trend in her second period ran parallel to a public desire for it.
However, she never indulged in salacious details and frank language as many of her contemporaries did; for she chose to assert
her independence once more by exercising a strict sense of dis-
crimination and selectivity. Unsavory topics such as dope addiction, adultery, illegitimate children, and vile old men have their
place in her fiction; but each is treated with discriminating
taste.

On the other hand, such books as *The Quick or the Dead?* and
Barbara Dering, while representing the growing Realistic movement in America, also ran counter to the very narrow sense of
public morality which prevailed in far larger measure than did
taste for the new Realism. So here again, she asserted her independence from a large segment of the reading public and might
rightly be considered a rebel who, as history has proved, was
ahead of her time.

A sense of independence also characterizes her treatment of
women, as reflected in the female protagonist who dominates
most of her plots. This heroine has her genesis in "A Brother to
Dragons"; grows up with the Princess and to a lesser degree with
the country's literary tastes; and is a prominent feature even in

Firedamp, the final novel. To trace her progress is to trace what to the Princess was the ideal of womanhood. This tradition began, appropriately, in the early stories with a dashing beauty of about twenty, filled with verve and tempered with compassion. She is seen as a young married woman struggling between cold reason and sentimentality in *The Quick or the Dead?* In *Barbara Dering,* reason has triumphed; and, as a fiery young intellectual, Barbara challenges the women of her own day to be independent thinkers and to face life squarely and not through late Victorian rose-colored glasses. *Seléné* and *The Golden Rose* show her being initiated into a deeper kind of love, demonstrating that the intellect should rule woman, and not the senses. *World's-End* and *Shadows of Flames* demonstrate woman's capacity for suffering and for loyalty. They condone divorce, but they also remind women of the war years that endurance is itself a reward. *The Queerness of Celia* reasserts that, unless woman is independent and has faith in her own abilities, she can never know real love. At the same time, however, it teaches that woman must not be overly egotistical and that self-evaluation is a virtue. Finally, *Firedamp* again reminds woman that she should endure; but it compensates by implying that she should have the freedom to act as her conscience dictates and that, once she has done so, she should feel fully justified for her actions.

Whether a product of, or a rebel against, the decades through which she lived, Princess Troubetzkoy expressed numerous opinions of her changing times. *Barbara Dering* stands as a classic statement of feminism at the end of the century. Militant feminists of the 1970's might do well to note these pronouncements, as they came from a woman who for all her rebelliousness remained feminine—loyal to the man she loved, noncombative toward men in general, and ever mindful of sweetness of demeanor and attractiveness of appearance.

Both *Barbara Dering* and *World's-End* advocate the responsibility that the privileged have to care for the needy; *The Queerness of Celia* gives a vivid picture of the success ethic in the 1920's and comments upon its crassness; and *Love-in-A-Mist,* really a comedy of upper-class American manners, shows what the rich of the late 1920's thought about Prohibition and sex and explores their morals. *Firedamp,* much in the fashion of the novels of Henry James, is a commentary upon the old-world ideal of an aristocracy which contains many closeted skeletons in addition to centuries of cultural background. Finally, to complete the James analogy, the Americans in the story are shown to have more integrity of character, for all their innocence, than do the British aristocrats.

There remains, finally, an overriding accomplishment which outshines any one of these: the Princess existed quite apart from her writings as a whole, a self-justified human being in her own right. Long before she let a word of anything she had written see print, she had existed as the person she was to transfer to fiction. This is something that can be said—or is said—of all too few writers. This fact deserves recognition even in this day of formalist criticism when aspects of an author's life are considered anathema. For, while these critics talk of the unimportance of biographical detail, their contemporary writers suffer from narcissism to the extent of changing their personal lives to coincide with the fictional images of themselves. It is a sad commentary on writers and critics alike when the writer fails to count as an entity, separate from his work, and even more sad when he is so weak as to be shaped by what he has created.

Robert M. Adams, in writing of John Milton, has sagely observed that the Puritan poet attempted throughout his career to "make his life a work of art in which is exemplified to the rest of us what the armed soul impelled by its own conscious destiny can endure and accomplish." [4] Thus may it be remembered of Princess Troubetzkoy: that before literature, and through it and above it as well, there was a life which was a conscious work of art—one exalted above that of most individuals and always majestic.

In suggesting a revival of interest in Princess Troubetzkoy to readers of the 1970's, one must consider her life and work both in terms of American literary history and of modern interests. Readers of today will doubtlessly feel an affinity with the independent spirit of her work mentioned above, especially in such rebellious examples as *The Quick or the Dead?* Also of current interest are her ideas concerning feminism, even though her concept of the liberated woman was nonpolitical and noncombative toward males. And the "flower children" of recent years should easily identify with *Seléné* and its exotic Esthete ambience, which is reminiscent of the milieu of Oscar Wilde and Aubrey Beardsley which they have apotheosized.

Of course, rebellion, feminism, and esoteric youth cults may prove to have been but passing fads; and succeeding generations may have to search for new touchstones of relevance. Literary history is more stable, however. Once informed with correct facts, it can be altered but little by time and taste. While its chronicle has already noted the contribution made to the Realistic movement by *The Quick or the Dead?*, it has lacked information in several key areas.

One obvious omission has been Princess Troubetzkoy's many associations among important literati of both Europe and America. Numerous examples of these relationships mentioned above invite further investigation. Far more significant, however, are two essential contributions peculiar to her own temperament and talent. First is her personal point of view, expressed both in fictional comment and personal action, and relating to the eventful period beginning in the mid-1880's and extending to 1930. Being trained upon both Europe and America for much of this period, this angle of vision was very nearly unique in its time, combining as it did traditional European cultural influences and an aristocratic southern heritage, but remaining free from any of the stringent limitations of either. The observations emanating from this vantage point sometimes paralleled popular attitudes, and at times rebelled fiercely against them; but as perceptive gauges of the times in which they were made, such comments should prove valuable to any observer.

A final contribution to Princess Troubetzkoy's native literature is seen in scattered places among the novels, poems, and dramas of both artistic periods, but most prominently and consistently in *World's-End, Shadows of Flames,* and *Firedamp:* her achievement in literary art alone. It is her accomplishment within this realm, which transcends both the confines of time and of history, that offers the most persuasive justification for her revival by the present generation and perpetuation by generations to come.

Notes and References

Chapter One

1. See, for example, "'Castle Hill,' the Home of Dr. Thomas Walker," *Kentucky Progress Magazine*, IV, 8 (April, 1932), pp. 23, 32–33, and "Castle Hill, Virginia, the Country Home of the Prince and Princess Troubetzkoy," *Country Life*, XXVI (October, 1914), 41–43.

2. John Hammond Moore, "Amélie Louise Rives and the Charge of the Light Brigade," *The Virginia Magazine of History and Biography*, LXXV, 1 (January, 1967), 89–96, has furnished a fine skeletal outline of the first Amélie Rives's life as well as the speculation that she might have been courted by Captain Edward Nolan who led the charge at Balaklava in 1854.

3. Unpublished autobiography of Judith Page Rives, p. 80; quoted by permission of Virginia Historical Society.

4. Of the four projected volumes of Senator Rives's *History of the Life and Times of James Madison* (Boston, 1859–68), only three were completed. Mrs. Rives's two best-known works were *Home and the World* (New York, 1857) and *Tales and Souvenirs of a Residence in Europe* (Philadelphia, 1842).

5. Unpublished autobiographical sketch, dated April 1, 1925; partially reprinted in Stanley J. Kunitz and Howard Haycraft, *Twentieth Century Authors* (New York, 1942), p. 1421.

6. *Ibid.*

7. In the archives of The Virginia Historical Society, Richmond.

8. Unpublished letter of April 12, 1886. This and other pieces of the correspondence are in the Harvard College Library.

9. Lizette Woodworth Reese, *A Victorian Village: Reminiscences of Other Days* (New York, 1929), p. 206; quoted in Jay Martin, *Harvests of Change: American Literature, 1865–1914* (Englewood Cliffs, 1967), p. 21.

10. See James D. Hart, *The Popular Book: A History of America's Literary Taste* (Berkeley and Los Angeles, 1963), especially pp. 157–200.

11. "A Brother to Dragons," *The Atlantic Monthly,* LVII (March, 1886), 302.

12. Good examples are "The Farrier Lass o' Piping Pebworth" and "Nurse Crumpet Tells the Story," which were ultimately published along with the initial story in book form as *A Brother to Dragons and Other Old-Time Tales* (New York, 1888).

Chapter Two

1. "The Farrier Lass o' Piping Pebworth," *Lippincott's Monthly Magazine,* XV (July, 1887), 127–57, and "Nurse Crumpet Tells the Story, *Harper's New Monthly Magazine,* LXXV, 448 (September, 1887), 620–633. (See above, Ch. One, n.12).

2. "Arnon," *Harper's New Monthly Magazine,* LXXV, 450 (November, 1887), 853–67.

3. "The Man of the Golden Fillet," *Lippincott's Monthly Magazine,* XLI (February, 1888), 241–71.

4. Though published later in 1888 under a separate cover, all references will be to the more accessible version in *Harper's New Monthly Magazine,* LXXVI (January, 1888), 189–235.

5. Hamilton Aïdé, " 'The Quick or the Dead?' and 'Virginia of Virginia,' " *Nineteenth Century Magazine,* XXV (February, 1889), 229.

6. *The Young Elizabeth,* her finest drama. Though never published, it was revised several times (see Robert W. Hungerford, "An Edition of Amélie Rives Troubetzkoy's 'The Young Elizabeth,' " unpublished master's thesis, the University of Richmond, 1969).

7. "Miss Amélie Rives's Novels," *The Saturday Review,* LXVII (April, 1889), 765.

8. *The Quick or the Dead?, Lippincott's Monthly Magazine,* XLI (April, 1888), 229.

9. William Dean Howells, *The Rise of Silas Lapham,* ed. with an introduction by Edwin H. Cady (Boston, 1957), p. 161.

10. Unsigned review, New York *Times,* November 18, 1888, p. 4.

11. John Hammond Moore, "The Vagabond and the Lady: Letters from Richard Hovey to Amélie Rives," *The Mississippi Quarterly,* XX (Spring, 1968), 139.

12. Ophélia Hives [pseud.], *Be Quick and Be Dead: A Parody with Apologies to Amélie Rives* (New York, 1888), p. 7.

13. Thomas Cooper DeLeon, *The Rock or the Rye* (Mobile, 1888), p. 7.

14. "Notes for a Biographical Sketch of Amélie Rives Troubetzkoy (Princess Pierre Troubetzkoy)," dated July 18, 1934, in the Alderman Library, the University of Virginia.

15. "Chronicle and Comment," *The Bookman,* XXXV, 4 (June, 1912), 354.

16. Edgar Fawcett, "A Few More Words About Miss Rives," *Lippincott's Monthly Magazine*, XLIII (September, 1888), 390. *The Quick or the Dead?* was by far her most reviewed title.

17. Warner Berthoff, *The Ferment of Realism: American Literature, 1884–1919* (New York, 1965), p. 9.

18. It should be noted, however, that a secondary reason for pushing the wedding day forward was the absence (in Panama) of Amélie's father, who disapproved of Chanler.

19. In addition to bound copies of *Monthly Magazine*, containing the novel which were released subsequent to April, 1888, Lippincott's published a book version in 1889.

20. See unsigned review, New York *Times*, October 2, 1888, p. 4.

21. Fawcett, p. 394.

22. *Herod and Mariamne*, *Lippincott's Monthly Magazine*, XLII (September, 1888), 310.

Chapter Three

1. According to Mrs. Edgar Dugdale, ed., *Chapters of Autobiography, by Arthur James, First Earl of Balfour* (London, 1930), p. 231, the name was given by Lord Charles Beresford.

2. Margot Asquith, *An Autobiography* (New York, 1920), II, 166.

3. The Right Honorable Earl of Ronaldshay, *The Life of Lord Curzon* (New York and London, 1927), I, 162.

4. Mr. and Mrs. Henry White. Mr. White was first secretary of the American embassy in London. (His wife had been a Chanler.)

5. Asquith, p. 23.

6. See Welford Dunaway Taylor, "A 'Soul' Remembers Oscar Wilde," *English Literature in Transition*, XIV, 1(1971), 43–48.

7. See Emily Clark, *Innocence Abroad* (New York, 1931), pp. 80–81.

8. *The Witness of the Sun* (Philadelphia, 1889), p. 95.

9. Unpublished will (copy) of Amélie Rives Troubetzkoy (Virginia Historical Society).

10. Unpublished letter from Louisa Pleasants, January 29, 1891 (Duke); quoted by permission.

11. The Baltimore *Times*, November 11, 1891, n.p.

12. In all, three installments appeared in *Cosmopolitan*: XI, 4 (August, 1891), 386–410; XI, 5 (September, 1891), 538–66; and XI, 6 (October, 1891), 732–60.

13. Unsigned review in *The Spirit of the Times*, October 31, 1891, n.p.

14. *Idem.*

15. Unsigned review, *The Nation*, LII (December 17, 1891), 260.

16. He was a partner in the firm of Chanler, [W. G.] Maxwell, and

[Harry Van Ness] Philip, located in the Equitable Building, 12 Broadway, New York City.

17. For instance, Miss Pleasants wrote him on December 14, 1891, from Hot Springs that Amélie had grippe and was "full of" malaria (Duke).

18. Thomas Hardy's *Tess of the D'Urbervilles* had appeared the year before.

19. *Barbara Dering* (Philadelphia, 1893), p. 242.

20. *Tanis, the Sang-Digger* (New York, 1893), p. 183.

21. Unsigned review in *Athenaeum*, No. 3449 (December 2, 1893), p. 767.

22. *Athelwold* (New York, 1893), p. 118.

Chapter Four

1. Emily Clark, *Innocence Abroad* (New York, 1931), pp. 78–79.

2. Rupert Hart-Davis, ed., *The Letters of Oscar Wilde* (New York, 1962), p. 340. (Hart-Davis's date of May, 1893 [given as problematic], should be some time in mid-to-late summer, 1894.)

3. Unpublished letter, April 24, 1895 (Duke); quoted by permission.

4. J. Bryan, III, "Johnny Jackanapes, the Merry Andrew of the Merry Mills: A Brief Biography of John Armstrong Chaloner [a spelling adopted by Chanler in later life]," *The Virginia Magazine of History and Biography*, LXXIII (January, 1965), 5.

5. *Ibid., passim.*

6. *The Nebraska State Journal*, March 8, 1896, p. 13; reprinted in Bernice Slote, ed., *The Kingdom of Art* (Lincoln, 1966), p. 334.

7. H. L. Mencken, *Prejudices: Second Series* (New York, 1920), p. 66.

8. Gerald Langford, ed., *Ingénue Among the Lions: The Letters of Emily Clark to Joseph Hergesheimer* (Austin, 1965), p. 35.

9. *Seléné* (New York, 1905), p. 41.

10. *Augustine the Man* (New York and London, 1908), p. 24.

Chapter Five

1. Slote, *op. cit.*, p. 335. (See above, Ch. Four, n.6).

2. *The Golden Rose* (New York and London, 1908), p. 11.

3. Nathaniel Hawthorne, *Mosses from an Old Manse*, II, in *The Complete Works of Nathaniel Hawthorne* (Boston, 1883), 535–36.

4. *Trix and Over-the-Moon* (New York and London, 1910), pp. 35–39.

5. *Pan's Mountain* (New York and London 1910), p. 211.

6. "Princess Troubetzkoy Discusses 'Saner Feminism,'" the New York *Times*, April 19, 1914, VI, p. 4.

7. Though identified by Julian Meade as Mrs. Walker (*I Live in Virginia* [New York and Toronto, 1935], pp. 146–47), other legends say the first Amélie Rives.

8. *Hidden House* (Philadelphia, 1912), p. 89.

9. The film, which also featured Booth Tarkington, George Ade, Ida Tarbell, and a number of lesser-known writers, was produced by the Actors' League of America in order to raise funds for helping unknown authors and to provide better protection for all writers under the existing copyright law. (See New York *Times*, February 8, 1914, V, p. 5.)

10. Interview with Edmund Archer, July 21, 1968.

11. Emily Clark, *Innocence Abroad* (New York, 1931), p. 82.

12. As the serial version is perhaps more accessible than the actual book, it can be read in weekly installments in *Collier's,* beginning with the November 29, 1913, issue.

13. Unsigned review, *Review of Reviews,* XLIX (June, 1914), 76.

14. Unsigned review, New York *Times,* April 6, 1914, VII, p. 206.

15. Slote, ed., *op. cit.,* p. 334.

16. Unpublished letter of July 20, 1914 (Alderman).

17. *Shadows of Flames* (New York, 1915), p. 49. (See above, Ch. Three, n.6).

18. Unsigned review, New York *Times,* September 15, 1915, V., p. 314.

19. Unsigned review, New York *Times,* January 26, 1920, p. 16.

20. Unsigned review, New York *Times,* November 2, 1920, p. 16.

21. Unpublished letter of June 8, 1932 (Alderman).

22. Benjamin Sledd, review of Armistead Churchill Gordon, ed., *Virginia Writers of Fugitive Verse* (New York, 1923), in *The Virginia Magazine of History and Biography,* XXXII (April, 1924), 206.

23. *As the Wind Blew* (New York, 1920), p. 79.

24. *The Sea-Woman's Cloak and November Eve* (Cincinnati, 1923), p. 23.

25. Unpublished letter of January 21, 1925 (Alderman).

26. *The Queerness of Celia* (New York, 1926), p. 102.

27. Joseph Wood Krutch, review in *The Nation,* CXXII (April 26, 1926), 484.

28. *Love-in-A-Mist* (New York, 1927), p. 95.

29. Clark, p. 83.

30. *Firedamp* (New York, 1930), p. 285.

31. Unsigned review, New York *Times,* February 16, 1930, IV, pp. 25, 27.

32. Unpublished letter of December 2, 1934 (Alderman).

33. Unpublished letter of October 11, 1931 (Alderman).

34. Unpublished letter of October 24, 1932 (quoted by permission

of Edmund Archer, to whose mother, Mrs. William Archer, it was sent).

35. Unpublished letter of August 29, 1935 (Alderman).

36. Unpublished letter of December 15, 1936 (Alderman).

37. Unpublished letter of August 25, 1937 (Alderman).

38. Unpublished letter of September 26, 1937 (Alderman).

39. Unpublished letter of December 1, 1937 (quoted by permission of Virginia Historical Society).

40. Robert W. Hungerford, ed., "An Edition of Amélie Rives Troubetzkoy's 'The Young Elizabeth,'" n.p. (unpublished master's thesis, the University of Richmond, 1969).

41. Arthur Sherbo, ed., *Johnson on Shakespeare*, VII in *The Yale Edition of the Works of Samuel Johnson*, p. 64.

42. Unpublished letter of December 24, 1942 (Alderman).

Chapter Six

1. Emily Clark, *Innocence Abroad* (New York, 1931), p. 83.

2. John Ruskin, *Modern Painters*, IV in *The Complete Works of John Ruskin* (New York, 1905), 159.

3. W. S. Gilbert, *Plays and Poems* (New York, 1932), p. 103.

4. Robert M. Adams, *Ikon: John Milton and the Modern Critics* (Ithaca, 1955), p. 223.

Selected Bibliography

PRIMARY SOURCES

1. Books
According to Saint John. New York: Lovell, Coryell & Company, 1891.
As the Wind Blew. New York: Frederick A. Stokes Company, 1920.
Athelwold. New York: Harper & Brothers, 1893.
Augustine the Man. New York and London: John Lane, 1906.
Barbara Dering. Philadelphia: J. B. Lippincott Company, 1893.
A Brother to Dragons and Other Old-Time Tales. New York: Harper
& Brothers, 1888.
A Damsel Errant. Philadelphia: J. B. Lippincott Company, 1898.
Firedamp. New York: Frederick A. Stokes Company, 1930.
The Ghost Garden. New York: Frederick A. Stokes Company, 1918.
The Golden Rose: The Romance of A Strange Soul. New York and
London: Harper & Brothers, 1908.
Herod and Mariamne. Lippincott's Monthly Magazine (special hard-
cover edition), XLII (September, 1888), 305–89.
Hidden House. Philadelphia and London: J. B. Lippincott Company,
1912.
Love-in-A-Mist. New York: Samuel French, 1927.
Pan's Mountain. New York and London: Harper & Brothers, 1910.
The Queerness of Celia. New York: Frederick A. Stokes Company,
1926.
The Quick or the Dead? A Study. Lippincott's Monthly Magazine
(special hardcover edition), XLI (April, 1888), 433–522.
The Sea-Woman's Cloak and November Eve. Cincinnati: Stewart Kidd
Company, 1923.
Seléné. New York & London: Harper & Brothers, 1905.
Shadows of Flames. New York: Frederick A. Stokes Company, 1915.
Tanis, the Sang-Digger. New York: Town Topics Publishing Company,
1893.
Trix and Over-the-Moon. New York and London: Harper & Brothers,
1909.

Virginia of Virginia. New York: Harper & Brothers, 1888. Also published in *Harper's New Monthly Magazine,* LXXVI (January,
1888), 189–235.
The Witness of the Sun. Philadelphia: J. B. Lippincott Company,
1889.
World's-End. New York: Frederick A. Stokes Company, 1914.

2. Stories and Articles
The following list is not exhaustive, but it contains all the stories
discussed in the text and an additional entry which, of all the stories
scattered through numerous periodicals, adds another dimension to
the author's achievement. The two essays have been chosen as being
truly representative and accessible to most readers.

"Arnon," *Harper's New Monthly Magazine,* LXXV, 450 (November,
1887), 853–67.
"Her Christmas Cabby," *Harper's Monthly Magazine,* CXXII (Decem-
ber, 1910), 94–107.
"Inja," *Harper's New Monthly Magazine,* LXXVI (December, 1887),
31–50.
"Innocence vs. Ignorance," *North American Review,* CLV (September,
1892), 287–92.
"The Man of the Golden Fillet," *Lippincott's Monthly Magazine,* XLI
(February, 1888), 241–71.
"Princess Troubetzkoy Discusses 'Saner Feminism,'" New York *Times,*
April 19, 1914, V, p. 4.

SECONDARY SOURCES

1. Books
ALDERMAN, EDWIN ANDERSON and JOEL CHANLER HARRIS, eds. *The
Library of Southern Literature.* New Orleans: The Martin and
Hoyt Company, 1909. Best single biographical sketch.
CHANDLER, MRS. WINTHROP. *Roman Spring.* Boston: Little, Brown
and Company, 1934. Contains a brief but poignant biographical
and critical section.
CLARK, EMILY. *Innocence Abroad.* New York: Alfred A. Knopf, 1931.
The chapter on Princess Troubetzkoy is one of the most impor-
tant, if loquacious, of all sources. Quite familiar and witty.
DeLEON, THOMAS COOPER. *The Rock or the Rye.* Mobile: The Gos-
sip Printing Company, 1888. Cleverest of all the parodies of *The
Quick or the Dead?*
LANGFORD, GERALD, ed. *Ingénue Among the Lions: The Letters of
Emily Clark to Joseph Hergesheimer.* Austin: The University of
Texas Press, 1965. Miss Clark, one of the founders of *The Re-*

viewer, makes frequent references in these chatty letters to the Troubetzkoys.

MANLY, LOUISE. *Southern Literature from 1579–1895*. Richmond: B. F. Johnson Publishing Company, 1895. Important evaluation of the Princess' first decade of writing.

MEADE, JULIAN R. *I Live in Virginia*. New York and Toronto: Longmans, Green and Company, 1935. Informal reminiscence of life at Castle Hill by a firsthand observer.

PAINTER, F. V. N. *Poets of Virginia*. Richmond: B. F. Johnson Publishing Company, 1907. One of the more valuable accounts of the Princess' abilities as a poet, though too early to be complete.

2. Articles

AÏDÉ, HAMILTON. " 'The Quick or the Dead?' and 'Virginia of Virginia,' " *Nineteenth Century Magazine*, XXV (February, 1889), 228–30. One of the best balanced of the early reviews, written during the heat of critical controversy.

"The American Widow—New Style," *The Saturday Review*, LXVI (December 17, 1888), 570–71. Typical of the early detractors—one-sided in its denunciation.

BORGMEYER, Charles L. "The Art of Prince Pierre Troubetzkoy," *Fine Arts Journal*, XXV, 6 (December, 1911), 323–35. The best biographical article on the Prince and a perceptive evaluation of his work, supported by clear illustrations. Continued in the next two issues.

BRYAN, J., III. "Johnny Jackanapes, the Merry Andrew of the Merry Mills: A Brief Biography of John Armstrong Chaloner," *The Virginia Magazine of History and Biography*, LXXIII (January, 1965), 3–21. Best source for information on the Princess' first husband; witty and occasionally profound.

FAWCETT, EDGAR. "A Few More Words About Miss Rives," *Lippincott's Monthly Magazine*, XLIII (September, 1888), 390–94. Vital article relating the early fiction to the current vogue of Realism.

HURRELL, J. D. "Some Days with Amélie Rives," *Lippincott's Monthly Magazine*, XLI (April, 1888), 531–36. Intimate account of the character and daily routines of the young authoress.

"Miss Amélie Rives's Novels," *The Saturday Review*, LXVII (June 22, 1889), 765–66. Important observation on developing style.

MOORE, JOHN HAMMOND. "The Vagabond and the Lady: Letters from Richard Hovey to Amélie Rives," *The Mississippi Quarterly*, XX (Spring, 1968), 131–43. Valuable as contemporary criticism of the years 1888–89.

TAYLOR, WELFORD DUNAWAY. "Amélie Rives: A Virginia Princess,"

Virginia Cavalcade, XIII, 4 (Spring, 1963), 11–17. First attempt at an overall evaluation, though primarily biographical and not literary.

————."A 'Soul' Remembers Oscar Wilde," *English Literature in Transition,* XIV, 1(1971), 43–48.

Index

In 1888, the year after her Newport debut, a youthful Virginia author named Amélie Rives (1863-1945) saw the press filled with news of her marriage to John Armstrong Chanler (a great-grandson of John Jacob Astor) and with sensational reactions to her first novel, *The Quick or the Dead?* Because the book sold over three hundred thousand copies, and because the marriage ended in a much publicized divorce in 1895, both incidents have been noted by literary and cultural historians. Less, however, is remembered of her second marriage to Russian portrait artist Prince Pierre Troubetzkoy (1864-1936); of the novels such as *World's-End* and *Shadows of Flames* which surpass *The Quick or the Dead?* in artistic achievement; or of her numerous plays which enjoyed successful Broadway runs in the 1910's and 20's.

This is the first book ever written on Amélie Rives. It offers a complete biographical survey as well as critical evaluations of all her book-length titles. It was undertaken in the belief that the subject's life and work both deserve being remembered and that, by attempting to cover both areas, she might be given a place in the literary consciousness of the present generation.

Material for the study was gathered from manuscript sources in many parts of the United States. Research was also done in the British Museum and in Northern Italy, where Dr. Taylor was able to interview the Principessa Mary Troubetzkoy, the last remaining member of the famous Troubetzkoy family.

Because the volume contains the most exhaustive amount of biographical and critical material of any source, it is hoped that it will become a standard work on the subject.